"I wish we had this book 20 years ago, but we are very lucky to have it going forward. Being a practical person, I gravitate toward work that helps me move the ball forward, and certainly **Animal Impact** is a classic."

- Esther Mechler, Founder, Spay/USA

"Effective animal advocacy is a difficult business. To move people with long-standing, entrenched attitudes and behaviors requires a deep understanding of what it takes to create change. This book will give you the insight you need to get the results you want."

- Che Green, Founder and Executive Director, Humane Research Council

"When it comes to the mantra 'Work smarter, not harder,' Caryn Ginsberg is the ultimate guru. Whether you're expanding an existing program or starting on a new endeavor, it would be a mistake to do so without referring to **Animal Impact** before moving forward. The difference means getting the most for the animals!"

- Ruth Steinberger, Founder, SpayFIRST!

"This book is a must read for grassroots animal activists everywhere. If you simply read the book, you will become familiar with tried and true practices and be inspired by how they were successfully used by some of today's most respected animal activists. If you use the book as a study guide and apply the knowledge learned, you'll get results you never dreamed possible."

- Bob Leonard, Cofounder, Mid-Atlantic Animal Rights Coalition

"This book will assist all of us in achieving and exceeding goals to help create or change laws to protect all creatures great and small."

- Belen Brisco, Animal Welfare Consultant

ANIMAL
IMPACT

Secrets Proven to Achieve
Results and Move the World

Caryn Ginsberg

PRIORITY VENTURES
Group
ACHIEVE IMPACT

www.priorityventures.com
Arlington, Virginia

Animal Impact: Secrets Proven to Achieve Results and Move the World

Free companion journal file available by request at **http://Animal-Impact.com/gift**
For additional tips, ideas, and recommendations for effective animal advocacy:

http://facebook.com/AnimalImpact

http://twitter.com/AnimalImpact

ISBN 978-0-9847660-7-9 (Paperbook)
ISBN 978-0-9847660-0-0 (EPub)
Library of Congress Control Number: 2011943201

Published by:
Priority Ventures Group LLC
1402 N Lincoln St., Suite 211
Arlington, VA 22201-4916
703.524.0024
http://priorityventures.com

Dedication

To you…
For believing in what's possible and doing everything you can to make it happen

To my husband, Michael Levitin…
Who believes in me and makes it possible for me to do what I can to help

Acknowledgments

More than 80 advocates shared success stories and lessons learned that make what follows compelling and powerful. These participants contributed to help other advocates enhance their effectiveness. Thanks to all of them, especially to Heidi Prescott for her foreword. Many of these leaders were quick to mention that they had people working with them who were integral to their accomplishments.

An amazing group of advisors and readers provided extensive, thoughtful feedback. They are Anthony Bellotti, Alexis C. Fox, Marsha Rakestraw, Kathy Savesky, and Bert Troughton. Che Green, Carol Glasser, and Kelley Tish Baker offered valuable assistance on selected chapters. Joan Dempsey, Sarah Speare, and Khalif Williams gave useful input on direction. I appreciate the time, expertise, and enthusiasm that each of them contributed.

The names of most participants appear in the main text. Others not mentioned but helping include Alexandra Bornkessel, Janet Enoch, Dulce Espelosin, Laura Flannery, Nicole Forsyth, Daniel Hauff, Paulette Lincoln-Baker, Reed Mangels, Julia Peirce Marston, Julie McCord, Margaret Ostafin, Andrew Rowan, Martin Rowe, Nathan Runkle, Joellen Secondo, Geeta Seshamani, Lindsey Siferd, and Zia Terhune.

I am grateful to people who helped me get started in animal protection: Adele Douglass, Alex Hershaft, Beth Preiss, Kathy Savesky, Ken Shapiro, Kim Stallwood, Zoe Weil, and the team at Humane Society University.

Neil Trent, Susan Sherman, and Sally Harte at the Animal Welfare League of Arlington hosted the photo shoot by Tomerlin Photography. Joan Mancuso and Samantha Ring provided photos of "coverdog" Harry, an adoptee from SPCA Tampa Bay. Lama Takruri assisted me in designing the cover, while Ann Marie Amico gave advice on graphics.

I was fortunate to work with my editor (and Mom), Maxine Ginsberg, a professional journalist. Scott Armstrong sparked my start then gave structure, ideas, and how-tos for the process. Sherry Essig and Joel Garfinkle also provided professional guidance that helped me see the opportunity. Friends Lynita Clark and Robert Opalacz offered unwavering support throughout the process.

Table of Contents

Foreword

I wish I'd known then what I know now and what you're about to learn.

I'd been with The Fund for Animals for three years when we staged a protest at the Hegins pigeon shoot in 1992 in conjunction with many other organizations. At this horrific and cruel event, shooters took target practice on hundreds of birds as they were released from boxes. Many of them were killed instantly. Some fell to the ground injured. Local youth tore the heads off these birds to finish them off, or piled them in trash cans to suffocate. Other wounded birds flew into the trees to die over hours or days.

Our goal was to attract as many demonstrators and as much media as possible to bring public attention to this appalling practice. Along with the protests, acts of civil disobedience brought more visibility to the event.

Fifteen hundred protestors descended on the town. Over a hundred were arrested for running on the fields to free birds before they were shot. We met our goal.

Or did we? The event raised awareness. But the disorganized, angry crowd of demonstrators distracted attention from the birds and the cruelty of the shoot. The media coverage focused on the tension between shoot supporters and opponents. Few articles mentioned the birds and their plight.

More people attended the shoot the next year. Hegins residents and businesses enjoyed an economic boost as more attendees paid to watch the macabre festivity. People who hadn't come previously showed up to see what the fuss was about. Even the Ku Klux Klan showed up to support the shoot. As more animals suffered and we were not getting anywhere, it was time to reassess.

The protest was a tactic* that emphasized conflict. To achieve our goal of stopping the shoot we needed a strategy,** a more comprehensive, integrated effort. We developed a plan to appeal to people's decency and compassion. Our approach addressed not just the public and the media but also elected officials.

---

* Tactic: "the specific actions, sequences of actions, and schedules you use to fulfill your strategy." [1]

**Strategy: "a plan of action designed to achieve a particular goal." [2]

For several years, we discouraged large-scale protests and instead focused on rescue and documenting evidence of violations of the cruelty statute. We sent trained veterinarians and volunteers to treat the wounded pigeons. They avoided any interactions with the crowd that could be perceived as violent or threatening. As a result, the media coverage changed significantly. Stories depicted the birds' suffering and violence by the shoot supporters. Reporters highlighted the senselessness of live pigeon shoots. Public sentiment began to shift.

We also strengthened our legislative outreach. Unfortunately, we may have actually missed opportunities to end the shoot earlier, because we didn't fully understand the needs of lawmakers. We didn't appreciate that inside negotiations and agreements are often essential to crafting a bill and garnering support.

However, our sophistication increased. We became very adept at targeting legislators who might have been on the fence by working with constituents and media in their districts. With more positive media, greater public support, and this thoughtful effort, we came within three votes of outlawing pigeon shoots in the state.

The campaign ultimately succeeded in the courts. Along the way, I gained experience about the importance of taking a strategic approach to make the very best use of our limited resources. It's not enough to *want* to do good for animals; we have to *do* good for animals. In addition to on-the-job training, I've read books about other movements, studied materials, and completed courses to discover the very best ways to affect change for animals.

In 2004 Mike Markarian, President of The Fund for Animals, and I asked Caryn Ginsberg to help us with strategic planning for our numerous campaigns and programs. At that time we felt like a great deal of our time and resources was spent "ambulance chasing" rather than proactively advancing an agenda. We certainly didn't have enough resources for everything we wanted to do, and we spread ourselves too thin trying to do too much.

Caryn guided a careful review of all our campaigns to determine which ones provided the best opportunities for us to help animals. In order to get the best results overall, we had to let go of some initiatives that were near and dear to our hearts. It wasn't easy. But just as we chose to abandon tactics that were unsuccessful during the Hegins campaign, we discontinued some projects that weren't the best use of time, energy, and funding. The disciplined approach she brought did more than help us evaluate our campaigns and programs. It became part of our ongoing work to choose new initiatives and craft effective strategies.

What you're about to read will help you develop approaches that work. You'll learn how to create change with the public, businesses, elected officials, government agencies, and other organizations. The information draws on Caryn's business background to reveal what companies know that we as animal advocates must know to motivate people to help rather than harm animals.

There are so many strategies and tactics in this book that I wish I'd known earlier in my animal protection work – perhaps more animals would have been saved from cruel treatment along the way. Thankfully, today young activists beginning their careers have access to information that will help them become more effective, leading to greater strides protecting animals, and there is greater focus today on planning.

This book includes comprehensive information that will help you get from point A to point B much quicker. My staff and I have used these methods in hundreds of campaigns focusing on issues such as dogfighting, cockfighting, fox-penning, canned hunts, fur, factory farming, and more.

You will find the information in this book useful and easy to implement. Refer to it often to plan any program, campaign, communications effort, personal outreach activity, or other initiative. Whether you are an individual advocate or part of a group, new to animal protection or a seasoned veteran, the approaches here can help you be more effective.

We share a passion for animals. I'm delighted that Caryn has written this book to share with you some of the very best ways to make the world better for them.

- Heidi Prescott, Senior Vice President, Campaigns, The Humane Society of the United States

Courtney L. Dillard originally recounted and analyzed the Hegins campaign in detail in "Civil Disobedience: A Case Study in Factors of Effectiveness," Society & Animals, Vol. 10, No. 1[3]

Introduction

You care deeply about helping animals. For all that you give and do, surely you deserve the very best help to be as influential as possible.

You <u>can</u> get better results from the time, energy, and money you already have. It doesn't matter where you're starting from today or which issue matters most to you. You can improve your impact whether you are a lifelong animal advocate or have gotten involved more recently.

Like many people new to animal protection work, I initially tried a variety of efforts: writing letters, staffing outreach tables, leafleting, helping in an organization's mailroom, visiting my political representatives, and occasionally attending a protest. Although I enjoyed taking action to spread animal-friendly messages, I didn't have the satisfaction of seeing much impact for my time and effort.

It wasn't that such activities are unproductive. Rather some of them seemed more useful than others. When I tabled to promote vegetarian eating at health fairs, for example, many people came to the table, eager to learn more about how they could take steps to eat more plant-based foods. When I spent time on Washington, D.C.'s National Mall, fewer of my interactions with passing tourists and residents were worthwhile. More often than not, it seemed, I ended up speaking with at least one animal-farmer here on vacation – not the most likely candidate for change.

While I enjoyed spending time with my fellow volunteers in both situations, I felt very differently about the two types of tabling. The health events were energizing. The time passed quickly and I was excited about the enthusiastic reaction I got. The Mall events left me drained.

I quickly decided that if I only had a certain amount of time to spend to help animals, I wanted to use that time as effectively as possible. I had a wealth of professional experience motivating people to take action. Could what I knew about strategy in the for-profit sector help people create more change for animals?

It could and it has. For over ten years I've had the privilege of helping people use proven techniques to accomplish more for animals. Through projects, as a speaker, and in articles, I've reached individual activists, volunteers, staff members at organizations large and small, board members, and funders. They have used the approaches I've shown them to get better results faster.

Now I've created a simple, powerful framework called the ACHIEVEchange system that you can use again and again for your personal activism, local programs, online presence, or national campaigns. The system and the detailed explanations combine my strategy background, my insight from working with animal protection advocates, and lessons from leading thinkers on creating change. These ideas can transform the effectiveness of your advocacy …and how you feel about the time you spend helping animals.

You'll see exactly how to work with these methods. I've included success stories from individuals, small groups, and leading organizations. These examples span the full spectrum of animal advocacy: sheltering, food issues, wildlife, and more. Although most of the stories are from the United States, some are from other countries. The principles apply around the world.

It doesn't matter if you agree with the issue in an example. Open admission shelters and no-kill facilities can learn from what the other does well. Promoting any form of vegetarianism shares much in common with advocating for more humane methods of raising animals for food. Advocates can use similar approaches to gain welfare reforms and to work toward abolition. Whether you refer to "pets" or "companion animals," "farm animals" or "farmed animals," I invite you to focus on lessons learned and how you can use them to create the change you want. As Timy Sullivan of PetFix Northeast Ohio notes:

> **If we partner only with those who are already on the same page, we… miss valuable opportunities to teach and learn.**[4]

The people who contributed stories are not necessarily on the same page with each other or with me on every issue, tactic, or philosophy. Yet, they agreed to take part in this collaboration to help convey an approach that can have a profound impact on our progress.

Of course, it was not possible to include every effective organization and individual. There are numerous other groups and people whose work I respect and that could have provided additional examples of top-notch advocacy.

Sometimes we'll look at less successful endeavors and how using the ACHIEVEchange system could have made a difference. These situations can offer our most powerful learning opportunities, so I heartily thank the individuals and organizations that have shared them. They'll tell you how they think they could have done better. When I point out ideas, I am building lessons learned from their work, not criticizing it.

Nor should you infer any criticism or feel any guilt if you look back at some of your past efforts and think you might have approached them another way. The poet Maya Angelou said some variation of "when we know better, we do better."

I applaud you for your commitment to being the most effective advocate for animals that you can be. I look forward to your success stories from using these techniques.

How to Get the Most Out of This Book

Please don't read this book

I like to joke that for someone who's read as many self improvement books as I have, I don't seem to have improved that much.

I finally figured out that that's because while I may read the books, I quickly forget most of what I've learned. Worse, I rarely put much of it into practice.

How about you? Have you read other books to improve your effectiveness in animal advocacy? How much of a difference have they made in what you're doing and the results you're getting? If you haven't read other books on animal advocacy, consider books you may have read to make other changes in your life, such as for diet, exercise, time management, organization, or financial management.

Fortunately for us all, there's a whole field about adult learning. It seems that as we get older, those tried and true methods of listening to lectures and reading books aren't always as effective as they used to be. The design of this book and the tips below will help you engage in ways that enhance the learning process and the results you'll get for yourself and animals.

1. **Complete the activities**. You'll find activities and questions to help you understand and apply the material. Take your time to think through them carefully. If you can't resist reading ahead, please plan a second pass to consider them in more depth. (Either way, reading the book multiple times can greatly enhance your new capabilities.)

2. **Take notes.** Writing down your responses, as well as other key impressions, will also help you retain more of the information. You can request a free companion journal file, a $9.95 value, at http://Animal-Impact.com/gift. Or just use a notebook. You'll have a summary document that's easy to revisit to remind yourself about takeaways that you want to act on in the future.

3. **Generate ideas.** As you're learning new points, jot down your thoughts on how to apply them in your advocacy. Don't worry about creating a perfect plan. Just capture ideas that you can use later.

4. **Buddy up.** Bert Troughton of the ASPCA notes that one of the best ways adults learn is through conversation. Ask a friend or colleague to read the book as well. By discussing the topics and how to apply them, you'll magnify your insight and ideas many times over.

5. **Take action.** In the final chapter, *Getting Started*, you'll find more about how to move from reading to doing. This is your jumping-off point to make what you've learned about more effective advocacy becomes part of your every day efforts. The *Resources* section at the end lists materials you might like to explore. When you request your free companion journal file, you'll gain access to online links to many of them.

These are just a few ways you can maximize what you get out of this book. Consider what works for you based on your learning style. Are you audio-inclined? Read out loud, if not the whole book, at least the points at the beginning of each chapter. Does it help you to form vivid pictures in your mind of how it would look to put these ideas into action? Would you do better to stand or move around while recapping what's most meaningful to you at the end of each chapter?

What you know now has helped you get here; what you continue to learn will get you where you are going.

- Ruth Thirtle, Business Development Specialist (proud adopter from DCH Animal Rescue, New South Wales, Australia)

You hold in your hands information that can transform your advocacy. I hope you'll put it to work to get the results you and the animals deserve.

Chapter 1

The Challenge

In this chapter:

- Faced with widespread animal suffering, resistance to change, and often-powerful opposition, we need to work smarter; the same old approaches will continue to yield the same old results.
- Nonprofits, government, and innovative individuals have adapted marketing approaches to advance change, such as reducing smoking and drunk driving, increasing voting and exercising, and fighting poverty and homelessness.
- This type of marketing is called **social marketing**. For our purposes, we can define social marketing as the use of commercial marketing approaches to influence people to voluntarily adopt a behavior that helps animals.
  - Social media is just one ingredient in social marketing's recipe for success.
- Some animal protection organizations are using social marketing to deploy common advocacy techniques, including social media, to greater effect.
- We in the animal protection community need to harness social marketing's power on a much larger scale if we want to see real results.

• • • • • • •

Every day advocates invest money, time, expertise, and energy to make the world better for animals. We achieve victories on some issues in some places, but experience setbacks elsewhere.

Have you talked to people, staffed a table at an event, handed out leaflets, attended a protest, used social media, advertised, run a campaign, or done other outreach? If so, you've probably experienced frustration when someone (or almost everyone) ignores or rebuffs your plea to help.

You work hard to get people to be kind and compassionate to animals. Why don't they always do what you ask?

Big Problems Are Hard Problems

It's very difficult to overcome societal norms and personal inertia. Unfortunately, animal suffering is vast and entrenched.

Consider these recent figures. In the United States alone:

- More than a million lab animals endured experimentation in 2009. Seventy-six thousand of them experienced painful procedures without receiving relief.[5]
- About 3 million healthy and adoptable cats and dogs were euthanized in shelters in 2010.[6] Others suffer in the streets or are victims of cruelty and neglect.
- 12.5 million people aged 16 years old and older hunted a variety of animals in 2006.[7] Over 100 million animals were killed for "sport" annually in the 1990s.[8]
- Nine billion-plus cows, pigs, sheep, chickens, turkeys, and ducks were killed for food in 2009.[9] For many of them, along with hundreds of millions of egg-laying hens, life pre-slaughter is a torturous existence with dark, crowded, unsanitary housing and terrifying, painful procedures.

These figures include only a few of the countless and varied ways animals suffer in just one country. Globally and for all types of animals, the magnitude of the problem is almost unimaginable.

We Face Powerful Opposition

The people, industries, and institutions working against the humane treatment of animals typically enjoy significant advantages, including far greater resources.

Even the largest organizations in our field are quite small compared to the entities that oppose them. For example:

- Sales of animals in 2011, including by pet shops and breeders, will total more than $2 billion, according to the American Pet Products Association.[10] That's over eight times the combined budgets that the American Society for the Prevention of Cruelty to Animals (ASPCA) and The Humane Society of the United States (The HSUS) had in 2009 to address a wide range of animal protection issues.[11]
- U.S. fur sales were $1.3 billion in 2010.[12]

- The annual budget of the National Rifle Association was $220 million in 2010.[13]
- The dairy industry has spent as much as $180 million a year on milk promotion.[14] That's more than the combined 2009 budgets for Farm Sanctuary, Physicians Committee for Responsible Medicine, Compassion Over Killing, Vegetarian Resource Group, Farm Animal Rights Movement (FARM), and Mercy For Animals.[15]

As you know, money brings power and influence. Industry can afford big advertising campaigns, publicity efforts to reach the media, and lobbyists to sway legislators.

We Have to Be Smarter

Simply showing up and kicking the ball harder and running faster isn't going to make you a winner.[16]

- Chris Cade, Think Without the Box

No matter how passionately we feel, how many times we repeat our arguments, or how strong the language we use, we may achieve little. We must become experts in how to create change. Many animal protection advocates are now employing more sophisticated approaches than in the past.

It's not all about money. Just like the story of David and Goliath, savvy animal protection advocates have moved giants like McDonald's, Trader Joe's, Hollywood celebrities, the U.S. Department of Agriculture, and the U.S. Congress to act for animals. In describing the historic campaign against Revlon by renowned animal activist Henry Spira, Peter Singer, author of Animal Liberation, asks:

Could there be a more unequal contest than this one, which pitted a high school teacher working out of his own apartment against the flagship of the cosmetics industry?[17]

- Peter Singer, Ethics into Action

Through careful strategy and persistent execution, Spira persuaded Revlon to provide $750,000 for The Rockefeller University to launch a multi-year effort to find alternatives to testing cosmetics in the eyes of rabbits. The campaign ultimately yielded another $1 million from Avon, Bristol Myers,

Estée Lauder, Max Factor, Chanel, and Mary Kay to create the Center for Alternatives to Animal Testing at Johns Hopkins University.[18]

While successes like these may garner widespread attention, equally important victories are happening at the local level. The shelter increasing adoptions, the activist winning a ban on circuses with animals in her community, and the person getting more veg options in his office cafeteria are all making important gains.

To do more with less, individual advocates, grassroots groups, community organizations, and national leaders have learned to work smarter. Many of them are borrowing from what businesses have known for years.

• • • • • • •

Paul Shapiro Learns to Maximize Results

Paul Shapiro grew up in an animal-loving household where the dogs were considered part of the family. His mother served on the board of directors of a local humane society and helped out at the shelter several days a week. After seeing videos of slaughter plants when he was 13, Paul became vegetarian (and later vegan) and began volunteering for animal advocacy organizations.

In high school, Paul started an animal protection club. The group brought in speakers and videos, and offered veg feed-ins for classmates. The club soon grew beyond the school grounds to become the D.C. grassroots group Compassion Over Killing (COK).

Paul believes that some of COK's first work was not as productive as it could have been.

> There were several years that we did things that felt good to do, but weren't actually effective in helping animals. I'm thinking about some of the raucous protests. We also did various sit-ins that led to the arrest of some folks. The intent was certainly to help animals, but I don't think we were introspective about whether we were tangibly helping animals.

Norm Phelps, former spiritual outreach director of The Fund for Animals, inspired Paul and his colleagues to become "teachers rather than fighters." COK shifted its focus to helping people in a more positive manner, such as through feed-ins and getting more veg options in restaurants.

Becoming less confrontational and more strategic gave Paul an edge in creating change. His successes have ranged from getting restaurants to put veg options on their menus to persuading Ben & Jerry's to switch to cage-free eggs. First with COK and now with The HSUS, his victories have helped millions of animals.

Paul hopes other animal advocates will learn from his early mistakes:

> **Too often animal activists do things that we initially feel good doing, but aren't necessarily the most effective way to help animals. We should treat [our advocacy] as seriously as if we were doing this for our own business that was intended to make money.**
>
> **Applying business principles is a good way to create tangible results for animals.**

• • • • • • •

Learning from Business

You might think we're not anything like businesses. Our mission is to help animals, and a company's goal is to make money. You may feel motivated by a call to serve and believe corporate employees only care about salary, status, and other personal outcomes.

What we have in common, though, is the need to get people to take action. For example:

- Animal protection advocates want people to adopt from a shelter or rescue group. Pet shops, breeders, and other for-profit outlets induce them to buy instead.
- We ask homeowners and local governments to use non-lethal approaches to deal with wild animals. Wildlife control firms convince them to use lethal methods.
- Activists endorse eating a plant-based diet or at least more humanely produced food. The meat, egg, and dairy industries promote consuming their products without regard for animal treatment.

If you think about the statistics we reviewed on the pervasive use of animals, it's clear which side is winning – business. Fortunately, the same approaches that businesses use can help us help animals. We can apply these methods in a positive, ethical way. Leading advocates are already doing so and getting better results.

"Good Marketing" Is Not an Oxymoron

One of the most important factors that separates business success from failure is effective marketing.

Many people equate marketing with advertising, especially with the advertising from enormous corporations. It's bad. Nonprofits can't afford to do it.

Advertising is part of marketing, but it's not all of it. **Marketing** is a process that businesses use to motivate people to enter into an **exchange**, usually spending money to get goods or services. Elements of the marketing process include:
- Setting goals
- Determining whom to serve
- Understanding what they want
- Developing goods and services (product)
- Setting charges (price)
- Selling through stores, online channels or other outlets (place)
- Creating and disseminating persuasive messages (promotion)
- Measuring results of campaigns and programs

We can use a similar marketing process to create an exchange. We want people to exchange their animal-unfriendly behaviors for animal-friendly ones. Using these marketing steps enhances our effectiveness with the money we have.

Isn't marketing about manipulation? Well, the company that makes the dog food you've chosen or promotes dissection alternatives is as engaged in marketing as are businesses that sell products you may dislike. Even a neighborhood lemonade stand engages in marketing.

Marketing is no more inherently "evil" than a knife. You can use a knife to whittle a toy, chop ingredients, or survive in the wilderness. But you can also slash a painting, kill someone, or cut the carelessly placed finger. In the same way, marketing is a neutral tool wielded for benefit or harm depending on the motivation and skill of those who use it.

We need to work as hard and, more important, as smart as the people on Wall Street work to sell stocks and as hard as advertisers work to sell the latest SUV.

Although our goals are different, the mechanisms of reaching other people and selling the message (in our case, of animal liberation) are well established....[19]

- Bruce Friedrich, "Effective Advocacy: Stealing from the Corporate Playbook"

Marketing Is a Tool for Social Change

In the last forty years, public health and environmental organizations have adapted what businesses know about marketing. They've prompted people to:

- Stop smoking
- Avoid driving drunk
- Recycle
- Exercise
- Vote

Individual advocates are also advancing exciting new initiatives based on principles of achieving behavior change.

- Canadian Shawn Ahmed left graduate school to start *The Uncultured Project*, an effort to reshape how people respond to global poverty and to bring concrete improvements to Bangladesh.[20]
- Mark Horvath, a former Hollywood insider who has also been homeless, created *Invisible People* to engage citizens, communities, and governments to take action to help the homeless in the United States.[21]
- Noha El-Bassiouny of Egypt markets to marketers! She launched *Ethics-Based Marketing* to influence people in companies, associations, and universities to use ethical principles to guide their marketing actions.[22]

There's a special name for marketing that's used to achieve societal good rather than to make money. It's called "social marketing." **Social marketing** means:

The use of marketing principles and techniques to influence a target audience to voluntarily accept, reject, modify, or abandon a behavior for the benefit of individuals, groups, or society as a whole.[23]

- Philip Kotler, Ned Roberto, and Nancy Lee, <u>Social Marketing: Improving the Quality of Life</u>

For our purposes, we can define **social marketing** as:

The use of commercial marketing approaches to influence people to voluntarily adopt a behavior that helps animals.

"Influencing people to voluntarily adopt behavior" can include not only getting the public to make new personal choices but also...

• Moving businesses and government agencies to change policy
• Persuading legislators to vote for pro-animal measures
• Engaging media to pursue animal stories
• Motivating supporters to volunteer time and donate

Why Haven't We Done More Social Marketing?

In their classic article "Social Marketing: An Approach to Planned Social Change," Philip Kotler and Gerald Zaltman described social marketing's purpose as "to help translate present social action efforts into more effectively designed and communicated programs that elicit desired audience response."[24] That article launched social marketing as a discipline in 1971.

The animal protection movement in the United States at that time consisted primarily of small, local organizations, often led by animal care or control experts rather than people with experience motivating people to change. The HSUS was still a fairly small organization.[25] Best Friends Animal Society (Best Friends) and People for the Ethical Treatment of Animals (PETA) did not exist.

Leaders in the emerging animal rights movement in the 1970s and 1980s were often strong personalities more prone to "charge the barricades" than to study the subtleties of influence strategies.[26] That wasn't necessarily all wrong. Alex Hershaft, President of FARM, describes three stages of issues within social movements. In the first, the Alert Stage, activities that draw attention are important to create public awareness. Heightening the visibility of animal issues was, therefore, valuable.

However, for a movement to succeed, it can't simply continue to generate awareness It must move on to the second stage, Discussion, where it builds agreement and then to the third stage, Reform, where it achieves action.

> The biggest pitfall [of the second stage, Discussion,] is that a lot of us are still stuck in the alerting stage.... We'll be in a situation where people want to come and learn more about our issues and we're still screaming, 'Meat is murder' and 'You're a puppy killer.' That's not very conducive to coming up and learning more about vivisection or eating animals. We have to be very careful. Are we trying to get a rise out of people or are we trying to inform them?
>
> ....
>
> The purpose [of the Reform Stage] is to introduce lasting change, to actually bring about changes in behavior... the pitfall in our movement at this stage is that a lot of us lose interest...[27]
>
> - Alex Hershaft, FARM

Some animal advocates have been slow to adjust their approach. Passion for animals and conviction that we're "right" can obscure the need to refine our methods.[28] The mistaken belief that social marketing is only for large organizations with bigger budgets discourages individuals and local groups.

However, simply adopting a social marketing mindset can dramatically enhance your work. You'll soon learn more about animal advocates who are using social marketing to make a difference on their own and in organizations such as Albert Schweitzer Foundation (Germany), Animal Welfare League of Arlington, ASPCA, Compassion in World Farming (UK), Compassion Over Killing, Delaware Action for Animals, The HSUS, Mercy For Animals, PetSmart Charities, Save Animals from Exploitation (SAFE, New Zealand), Vegetarian Resource Group, and Wildlife SOS (India). Outcomes have included:
- Increasing spaying and neutering
- Gaining veg options in restaurants and cafeterias
- Securing safer passage for wildlife
- Stopping plans to expand beaver hunting
... and much more.

Social Marketing Is Not Social Media

These days many people confuse social marketing with social media. Social media includes Facebook, Twitter, blogs, and other online communications that enable user-generated content and peer-to-peer sharing, often in real time. That's only a small part of social marketing, which existed long before social media.

Social marketing consultant Mike Newton-Ward compares social media to a carrot in the stir-fry of social marketing.[29] Other ingredients come from business marketing, including defining:

• What behavior you want people to adopt
• Which people you're addressing
• What they want
• What to say and how to say it (promotion)
• What else you need to do (product, price, place)
• How you'll know if your efforts are working

Social media is part of promotion to support the success of programs, campaigns, and other outreach. Even if you are an individual who blogs or works largely through Facebook and Twitter, social marketing will help you get better results from your efforts.

> **Social media without a strategy is a trick not a tool. So you have to present with excellence, and you have to have goals, reasons, and a strategy to make it effective.**
>
> **- Mark Horvath, Invisible People**[30]

• • • • • • •

A Life-Changing Moment for Aimee St. Arnaud

Aimee St. Arnaud knew as early as age six that she wanted to do something to help animals. As a teen, she volunteered at a shelter and for a wildlife ballot initiative.

To find work in the field, Aimee attended conferences and made sure to introduce herself to people. She landed a position with her local humane society after the executive director noticed her persistence in volunteering and attending events. Through additional networking and her ongoing work, she was invited to join Best Friends, where she was involved in the No More Homeless Pets campaign.

Conferences were the place not only to make contacts but also to get new ideas. At a Spay/USA gathering, Aimee heard Kathy Savesky talk about social marketing. When Kathy was executive director of the Peninsula Humane Society (PHS) in San Mateo, California, she read <u>Marketing Social Change: Changing Behavior to Promote Health, Social Development, and the Environment</u> by Alan Andreasen, another leader in the social marketing field. She used what she learned about social marketing to save more animals at PHS. She then pioneered social marketing in the animal protection field, including through her breakthrough article "Selling Your Organization's Messages."[31]

Aimee described the session as life-changing. Social marketing offered a powerful new approach for helping animals.

> When we look at animal welfare, it seems big and overwhelming. We look at [it] as being so different from anything else. Sometimes we get paralyzed....
>
> We don't like to be thought of as a business. But if you look at the different social movements and businesses, they're very aware of [what motivates people to change.] They do a lot of research. It's important to start looking outside our field....
>
> We can do all the programs in the world, but if we're not reaching people with the right message in the right language, we're never going to [achieve] what we want. If we were McDonald's or Target, we'd know how to reach them.

Aimee has put social marketing to work on many fronts, including as founder of the spay/neuter group Humane Ohio. Social marketing taught her and colleagues to ...

> re-think our judgments because we were operating on a premise from years in this field that people didn't care and didn't want to fix their pets. We've come to realize that the majority of people do want to fix their pets and are grateful for our services. They were facing barriers like cost and accessibility that made it hard for them. We've removed those barriers by doing special promotions, providing transport, and using a variety of ways to reach them from social media, such as Facebook and craigslist, to traditional media, including TV, radio and print.
>
> We have realized we also need to get out in the community, so we do a lot of grassroots door to door and events in the areas we are trying to reach. If you aren't talking to the people you are trying to reach, how do you get to know what motivates them?
>
> It can be uncomfortable to step outside our [comfort] zone, but incredibly rewarding. As a result, we currently fix over 12,000 animals a year and have a three-month waiting list, with plans to expand to 15,000 a year because of demand.

• • • • • • •

Whatever You Call It, It Works

Some of the success stories you'll read in the pages ahead are from people who, like Aimee and Paul, think explicitly about using practices from social marketing or business. Other examples come from people who don't think that way about what they do, but go about their efforts with similar consideration and insight. The "Ten Ways to Make a Difference" that Peter Singer summarizes from Henry Spira in Ethics into Action are consistent with social marketing. Spira's approach came from experience in a variety of social movements.

Are you enthusiastic about marketing, especially social marketing, as a powerful tool to help animals? If you're still uncomfortable with the term, please don't let that stand in your way. I've taken key points from social marketing and organized them into an easy-to-remember ACHIEVEchange system. You can use it to plan and execute effective initiatives for animals. The chapters that follow explain the framework and how to put it to work to enhance your advocacy.

• • • • • • •

The ACHIEVEchange System

Action and Audience

Our goal is changing behavior. Think of people as customers for change and address their "What's in it for me?"

Create Benefits and Cut Barriers

People change their behavior when they perceive the benefits of doing so to exceed the barriers.

How to Say Something to Someone Instead of Nothing to Everyone[32]

One size does not fit all. Choose the best people to target and tailor your efforts to them.

I Am Not My Target Audience

You don't think the same way as the people you're trying to influence. Listen to them to understand the best motivators.

Education Isn't Enough

It takes more than telling people about a problem to inspire them to act. Build your efforts considering product, price, place, and partnerships as well as promotion.

Voice Matters

How you say it is as important as what you say. Positive change begins with you.

Evaluate, Don't Guess

We have to determine if we're getting results and learn from our experience to do better.

If Madison Avenue can get us to buy things that are too expensive, don't taste good, and make us sick, why can't we use those same secrets to get people to do things that are good for them and animals?

- Kathy Savesky

• • • • • • •

Brad Shear Uses Business Savvy to Get the Job Done

Brad Shear worked in restaurants after college to pay the bills, but quit because it wasn't fulfilling. He answered an ad for kennel and front desk help at a shelter. He worked his way up to front desk supervisor and later to director of operations at a larger shelter.

When Brad joined Mohawk Hudson Humane Society (MHHS) as executive director, he set about enhancing the organization's image, a key aspect of marketing. At the time, there wasn't a lot of attention paid to the experience visitors were having at the shelter. Facility odors and procedures that were normal for staff and volunteers were off-putting to would-be adopters.

With his early experience in the hospitality industry, Brad knew that customer experience was critical. In an earlier position with Boulder Valley Humane Society, he'd partnered with the Dumb Friends League (Denver) to become an instructor for a customer service training program that a pet food manufacturer helped develop. He brought this training to MHHS. He also made people skills a key criterion for new hires, favoring applicants with customer service backgrounds from any field.

As a result, the organization became more customer-focused and improved its reputation. In 2010 when the ASPCA announced its new $100K Challenge, with a cash award for the U.S. shelter entrant that most increased the number of lives saved compared to the prior year, Brad felt MHHS was ready to tap into community pride and take its place among the leading humane groups nationally.

To do so, he once again turned to best practices from business. Brad and his team considered which local organization, in any industry, did the best job of marketing and advertising. They approached the law firm of Martin, Harding & Mazzotti LLP for advice on new ways to motivate adoptions. The partners not only agreed to help but also brought in their advertising agency and worked with a TV station to produce and distribute a 30-second public service announcement. One partner visited area radio stations to talk about hosting an adoption clinic and urged other businesses to do the same.

Brad and his team even borrowed from the famous "Got Milk?" campaign. Soon their "Got Pets?" signs, like the ones you see for political candidates, were all over New York's Capital Region.

MHHS adopted out nearly 400 more animals for August to October 2010 compared with the same period in 2009. Brad and his team finished in the top 10 for lives saved in the Challenge. MHHS was also among the three finalists for the $25,000 community engagement prize, beating out many larger shelters on both dimensions.

• • • • • • •

Achieve Impact

Please turn your new insight into action and impact by answering the following questions before you move ahead. I suggest you do this at the end of each chapter to make sure you capture what you think can best help you help animals. Remember you can request your free journal file at http://Animal-Impact.com/gift that lists the questions in each chapter.

1. What are two examples of marketing you see around you? Consider any effort that's intended to influence you to buy a product or service, engage in healthy behavior, adopt an environmentally-friendly practice, or take a civic action. You'll probably find you're on the receiving end of a lot of marketing from businesses, nonprofits, and government.

2. In each of these two examples, is your reaction positive or negative? What makes it so... the source? ...the product or behavior that's promoted? ...the message or images used? ...something else?

3. If you reacted negatively to how the marketing was done in one of your examples, how can you avoid having a similar impact in your advocacy? For example, if you felt a marketing effort was disrespectful, how can you ensure that you come across as respectful?

Also note key points or ideas you got from this chapter.

Chapter 2

Why People Don't Get it and What You Can Do

In this chapter:
- Being at the receiving end of a hypothetical advocacy campaign provides insight on how to be more effective.
- Introduction to the ACHIEVEchange system

• • • • • • •

Whether you're helping dogs and cats in your community, advocating for businesses to change their policies, pressing for government to pass laws, or working on any other of the seemingly endless animal protection challenges, you want to know what to say, how you should say it, and what else you should do.

But before we talk about you, let's talk about the people you're trying to influence on behalf of animals: family, friends, colleagues, community members, businesspeople, elected officials, government workers, or any other individual.

You know, THOSE people. Those people who listen to you or read your materials about dog and cat overpopulation, puppy mills, factory farming, fur, vivisection, shark finning, or other animal use and abuse and STILL keep doing what they're doing. It's painful. It's so obvious to you that what's going on is cruel and has to stop, but they won't get on board.

You may feel disappointed, discouraged, upset, or even angry at their seeming indifference to suffering. Do you complain to your fellow animal advocates about how horrible these people are? Maybe you just throw up your hands and wonder what is WRONG with them!

Why don't they get it?

Put the (Non-leather) Shoe on the Other Foot

You're used to talking to others about animal issues. You know how strongly you feel. How would you feel, though, if someone were talking to <u>you</u> or sharing written materials about a different type of issue?

Let's find out. You'll get some great insight on your advocacy and how to have more impact.

Two examples follow. They are:
- Asking you to stop shopping at malls or large retailers for clothing
- Telling you to eat only 100% raw vegan food

We'll refer back to this activity throughout the book. So please take a few minutes to consider the examples and jot down some notes on your response. You'll learn the most by doing both examples and truly engaging. I hope you'll have some fun with it, too!

For each example, imagine that someone is speaking to you or that you're reading a flyer or website. Be very aware of what you're thinking as you read the appeal to change. You'll find questions following each example to help you evaluate the experience.

(Do you already avoid buying clothes from traditional sources and eat 100% raw vegan food? If so, think about another potentially world-friendly or personally beneficial activity that you haven't undertaken, such as giving up your car, composting, installing solar panels, or working out regularly. What might an advocate for that behavior say to you?)

• • • • • • •

Example 1: The Evils of Shopping at Malls and Large Retailers

Shopping at the mall or in national retailers hurts the environment and people. It's important that you never buy clothing in these stores!

You may think cotton is 100% natural, but it actually depletes the soil. Unless it's organic, it's probably been treated with pesticides. These pesticides, along with fertilizers, end up in the water.

Synthetic fibers are produced using petrochemicals. "Dyeing and printing consume vast amounts of water and chemicals, and release numerous volatile agents into the atmosphere that are particularly harmful to our health."[33]

There's even more pollution when the clothes move by boat or truck or both to their final destination, so you can buy them.

It's not just an environmental issue. Manufacturers source a lot of clothing from China, where workers endure long hours. "Health and safety conditions in the factories include exposure to toxic chemicals, fire hazards and high risk of industrial accidents."[34]

When you buy new clothing from mass merchandisers you're supporting abuse and damaging the environment. You don't want to do that do you?

Actually, it's not just clothing. You really should stop buying pretty much anything from these places. Whether you buy kitchenware, electronics, or furniture, you're definitely damaging the environment and probably harming people as well.

• • • • • • •

Are you ready to give up buying anything in malls or major retail stores? Shoes? Bathing suits? Underwear? Bedding?

Consider these questions:
• Why did the example succeed or not succeed in convincing you to take action to avoid mall and national retail store shopping?
• If you weren't convinced, how might a different appeal have been more effective?

• • • • • • •

Example 2: The Importance of Eating 100% Raw Vegan Food

A vegan raw food diet includes fruit, vegetables, nuts, seeds, and grains, none of which is heated above 118 degrees. When you cook food above that temperature, you destroy the enzymes in it that help with digestion. You fundamentally alter its make-up. It's unnatural. Does any (nonhuman) animal cook its food?

Processing cooked food taxes your digestive system, ages you, and promotes disease, including cancer and heart disease. It's poison, really.

When you eat only raw food, you'll feel more energetic, have better-looking skin, and avoid the horrid sicknesses that plague so many people.

It can also be good for the environment if you eat raw food. Fresh fruits, vegetables, and nuts require little or no packaging, so you waste less paper, plastic, and ink when you buy them. Because you don't cook, you' don't need as much electricity or gas. Both electricity and gas production harm the planet. A lot of fruit comes from trees or bushes, so there's less soil loss from pulling up plants, another benefit for the Earth. In addition, with fruit, you don't even kill the plant.

Therefore, you really owe it to yourself and the world to give up cooked food and eat only raw food.

• • • • • • •

How'd we do this time? Are you ready to begin eating only raw vegan food? No? Ask yourself:

- Why not?
- What would it take to convince you?
- If you think there's no way you'd commit to raw vegan forever, is there an appeal that would get you to try in some way?

It's Not That You Didn't Get It… It's That You Didn't Want It

If you're like most of the people with whom I've shared these examples at conferences and training sessions, you're not ready to give up buying new clothes and home furnishings from major retailers. You're not making plans to start eating only raw vegan food.

The examples noted how you might be harming the environment or even other people with your choices. Because you're a compassionate person, I bet that mattered to you. But not enough.

Maybe you would never have considered either of these changes. More likely, however, the appeal wasn't compelling enough to make you even seriously contemplate taking action. If you're feeling uncomfortable, judged, or even hostile after reading the examples, how does that affect your willingness to consider the proposed change?

I hope from this activity you appreciate how a well-intentioned, passionate advocate for good can launch an effort that gets little or no results and even drives people farther away from the intended behavior.

• • • • • • •

Making Life Bearable

You may have felt that substantially changing your shopping or eating habits was too drastic. How about if you had to give up your income?

That's what animal protection advocates learned they were asking when trying to stop "dancing bears" in India.

For centuries, Indian sloth bear cubs have been violently and illegally poached from the wild. Members of the Kalandar tribe buy the young bears, whose mothers are often killed, to use as a form of "entertainment." To condition the bears to "dance" on command, handlers first remove the bears' teeth or file them down. Then they pierce the animals' sensitive muzzles and run a rope through the hole.[35]

Estimates of the dancing bear population ranged from 1,000 to 1,200 animals with about 100 to 200 cubs illegally poached from the wild each year. A variety of animal protection organizations worked with police and wildlife officials who had authority to confiscate the bears, who went to newly established sanctuaries.

The World Society for the Protection of Animals (WSPA) had worked with governments to eliminate dancing bears in Turkey and Greece, but found itself in a different situation working in India.

> While outright confiscation was a legal option, it presented a problem in India: most bear owners had no other way to make money and support their families. Without other options to earn a livelihood, owners were likely to poach a new bear from the wild to replace a confiscated one.
>
> It was important for us to acknowledge that this wasn't simply an animal welfare issue but also a case of humans being dependent on animals for their livelihoods. So, we decided to make our campaign more holistic by addressing the human aspect, and began working with bear owners to find them legal and cruelty-free livelihoods.
>
> - Sharanya Krishna Prasad, WSPA

WSPA, Wildlife SOS, and other international partners offered training and incentives to help the Kalandars engage in other work. After repeated efforts to convince them, the handlers started surrendering their bears and committing to alternative livelihoods.

> We convinced the Kalandars that 300 years of bear dancing had given them no progress, but by accepting this offer of rehabilitation, they would definitely see an improvement in their quality of life. This was an offer they could not afford to miss, especially since here was an option to move to a legal way of life and stop running from the law.
>
> - **Kartick Satyanarayan, Wildlife SOS**

Former bear handlers are now growing crops, weaving carpets, selling groceries, tailoring, and operating taxis. About 45 former handlers work for Wildlife SOS at their bear rehabilitation centers.

Comments from retrained Kalandars reflect the importance of a solution that addressed their needs.

> It was a risky existence earlier where there was no guarantee of income and also no guarantee that we would not be arrested by the police, as this was an illegal practice. Our lives have changed drastically. I can now support my family without fear and live a life of dignity.[36]
>
> - Imam

> It is hard to make a living for my family… Some days I earned more with [my bear] than with my taxis, but I know I am not going to be arrested for keeping a bear illegally and for the first time ever my children are getting an education. I'm proud to be able to give them this.[37]
>
> - Mohamed

These efforts have led to the rescue of 600 bears and helped the Kalandars and their families live better lives. Whether there may be a few dancing bears in outlying rural areas or whether this practice has been eliminated is uncertain, but both bears and people have benefited dramatically.

• • • • • • •

You Have to Have a Process

So how do you get the best results for animals while considering people? As the shopping, raw foods, and dancing bears examples, as well as your own experience, demonstrate, explaining what you believe is wrong or what you think is right isn't enough. You have to have a strategy.

> **You can't just say, 'This is a good thing' and expect it to just happen. You have to have a process by which good ideas become effective ideas.**
>
> **- John Hadidian, The HSUS**

> **Developing tactics in isolation from a strategy is one of the most common mistakes activists make, and it spells death for a campaign.**
>
> **- Melanie Joy, <u>Strategic Action for Animals</u>**[38]

You can use the ACHIEVEchange system to avoid the mistakes you've seen in these examples.

Let's see how the shopping and raw foods examples failed on each aspect of the system.

Action and Audience

Our goal is changing behavior. Think of people as customers for change and address their "What's in it for me?"
The examples talked at you; they didn't speak to you. They didn't provide what you needed to feel good enough to make a switch.

Create Benefits and Cut Barriers

People take action when they perceive the benefits of doing so exceed the barriers.
Although each appeal cited positives to the recommended action, they weren't big enough to make a difference. You probably also came up with many objections that weren't handled.

How to Say Something to Someone Instead of Nothing to Everyone

One size does not fit all. Choose the best people to target and tailor your efforts to them.
Everyone got the same generic message here. There was no customization to your current beliefs or practices.

I Am Not My Target Audience

You don't think the same way as the people you're trying to change. Listen to them to understand the best motivators.

Maybe the hypothetical advocate behind these appeals found the points compelling, but you didn't.

Education Isn't Enough

It takes more than telling people about a problem to inspire them to act. Build your efforts considering product, price, place, and partnerships as well as promotion.

These examples did little more than alert you to issues about what you do now and then ask you to change. Many of your objections were likely around the clothing or food (product), the time or emotional cost of change (price), or where you'd have to shop (place).

Voice Matters

How you say it is as important as what you say. Positive change begins with you.

The tone and style in these appeals left a lot to be desired. Would you like or trust someone who approached you this way? Probably not.

Evaluate, Don't Guess

We have to determine if we're getting results and learn from our experience to do better.

If I were using these examples in real campaigns, I'd want to know if they were having the intended result or not. Otherwise, I'm wasting time and money and doing less than I could to help.

Effectiveness Begins with Awareness

These shopping and raw foods examples often drive a profound perspective shift. When we put that proverbial shoe on the other foot and spend time at the receiving end of advocacy, we learn about what happens for the people we seek to influence.

The ACHIEVEchange system can help you avoid the pitfalls you've experienced and get dramatically better results for animals. In the next chapter, we'll look at how two successful efforts map to the ACHIEVEchange system. Then you'll learn about each step in detail with more examples to help you put it to work.

• • • • • • •

Achieve Impact

1. What were the most important ideas you learned from reading this chapter and completing the activity?

2. What initial thoughts do you have on how you might apply these ideas to get better results for animals?

Chapter 3

Effective Action

In this chapter:
An adoption program and a cage-free egg campaign illustrate how the ACHIEVEchange system works.

• • • • • • •

In the last chapter, you learned about the ACHIEVEchange system and saw how failure to follow the key elements weakened the appeals to change your shopping or eating habits. Now let's look at two cases of effective action and see how each effort included elements that map to the system. The success stories are simplified, but you'll begin to understand how to put the process to work.

Meet Your Match® with Dr. Emily Weiss

Dr. Emily Weiss was always interested in animals. In college, she had a mentor who encouraged her to become a behaviorist. She's studied everything from mice to elephants to Komodo dragons. As the ASPCA's vice president of shelter research and development, her work ranges from developing enrichment programs for animals in shelters to answering questions for the ASPCA's *Ask the Expert: Horse Behavior* column.

In 2008, she received the Tony La Russa Animal Rescue Foundation's Evie Award. The award recognizes individuals for their excellence in compassionate care of companion animals. DogChannel.com headlined its story "Creator of Unique Dog Adoption Program Awarded."[39] That title refers to the Meet Your Match® adoption program that Emily developed for dogs and cats.

The Meet Your Match program is an example of putting together all the pieces of effective social marketing to save animals' lives.

Action and Audience

Our goal is changing behavior. Think of people as customers for change and address their "What's in it for me?"

The goal of the Meet Your Match program is to save lives by increasing the number of adoptions, both by bringing in more people and by reducing the number of animals returned as unsuccessful placements. The program can get more animals into homes more quickly, reducing the amount of time dogs and cats stay in the shelter and the number euthanized.

The shelters use the Canine-ality® and Feline-ality® testing that Emily developed to assign each animal to one of nine categories based on activity level, interaction, vocalization, and more. People wanting to adopt complete a simple questionnaire about their experience with animals, expectations regarding social interaction, preferences for behaviors such as vocalization and play, and home environment. The survey includes questions such as:

- *I would consider my house to be like*: A library / Middle of the road / A carnival
- *I am comfortable with a cat that likes to play "chase my ankles" and similar games*: No / Somewhat / Yes
- *I want my cat to enjoy being held:* Little of the time / Some of the time / Most of the Time

Whether we are trying to adopt more animals, spay and neuter more animals, or increase the likelihood that pets will stay in the home, we must take the time to learn about our audience and come from their perspective.[40]

- Dr. Emily Weiss

Both potential adopters and shelters are audiences.

Adopters: The program addresses adopters' needs by helping them select an animal more likely to become the ideal companion.

Shelters: Shelters meet their need to place more animals. They can also enjoy the satisfaction of knowing that the animal has better odds of a loving, long-term home.

cat adopter survey

first name		last name			date		
address		city			state		zip
home phone ( ) -		work phone ( ) -			email		

1	I would consider my household to be like	A library	Middle of the road	A carnival	
2	I am comfortable with a cat that likes to play "chase my ankles" and similar games	No	Somewhat	Yes	
3	I want my cat to interact with guests that come to my house	Little of the time	Some of the time	All of the time	
4	How do you feel about a boisterous cat that gets into everything?	Love them but rather not to live with them	Depends on the situation	Fine by me	
5	My cat needs to be able to adjust to new situations quickly	Not important	Somewhat	Yes	
6	I want my cat to love being with children in my home	It's not important whether my cat loves being with children	Some of the time	Most of the time	Children do not often come to my house
7	My cat needs to be able to be alone	More than 9 hours per day	4 to 8 hours per day	Less than 4 hours per day	
8	When I am at home, I want my cat to be by my side or in my lap	Little of the time	Some of the time	All of the time	
9	I want my cat to enjoy being held	Little of the time	Some of the time	Most of the time	
10	I need my cat to get along with (circle all that apply)				Dogs Cats Birds Other
11	My cat will be	Inside	Inside and Outside	Outside	
12	I have lived with cats before	No		Yes Date_____	Currently
13	I prefer my cat to be talkative	No		Yes	It's not important if my cat is talkative
14	I want my cat to play with toys	Little of the time	Sometimes	Often	
15	I want my cat to be active	Not very active at all	Somewhat	Yes, very	

16 It is most important to me that my cat _____
   (fill in the blank)

FOR OFFICE USE ONLY	RECOMMENDED COLOR MATCH: PURPLE ORANGE GREEN
	RECOMMENDED FELINE-ALITY™(IES) _____

Create Benefits and Cut Barriers

People take action when they feel the benefits of doing so exceed the barriers.

Adopters: Research shows that barriers to adoption include not finding the right breed or type of animal, not knowing what to expect from shelter animals, and lack of knowledge or even wariness about the adoption process.[41] The Meet Your Match program addresses these barriers and provides additional benefits. By helping adopters identify a dog or cat more likely to fit their lifestyle, the process provides a more useful predictor than breed information does about what to expect. The process is fun and easy. The Richmond SPCA, one of many shelters that put the survey online, states under dog adoptions:

> **The Meet Your Match Canine-ality Adoption Program helps you find the dog that's right for you. Our dogs are assessed to determine characteristics. This Canine-ality Assessment takes the mystery out of the selection process by reliably predicting how a dog is likely to behave when he or she arrives in your home.**
>
> **- Richmond SPCA website**[42]

Shelters: In addition to increased adoptions, reduced euthanasia, and shorter length of stay for animals, benefits can include higher staff and volunteer morale. The program may also generate media interest. Of course, any new program takes time, requires change, and faces potential resistance from personnel (barriers). The Meet Your Match program, therefore, includes information, training, and support designed to make the process as smooth and easy as possible.

How to Say Something to Someone Instead of Nothing to Everyone

One size does not fit all. Choose the right people to target and tailor your efforts to them.

Adopters: A study by the Ad Council for The Humane Society of the United States and Maddie's Fund suggested that 41% of people planning to acquire an animal in the coming year, approximately 17 million people, had not adopted from a shelter in the past, but were open to the possibility. These people were termed "Swing Voters."[43] The Meet Your Match program can help "convert" some of this segment. It appeals to people within this group who believe dogs and cats have different temperaments, and so some will be better companions for them than others.

Although the adopter is free to choose any dog or cat, the process identifies a subset of animals most likely to fit each adopter's situation and preferences. Once the adopter completes the questionnaire, a shelter counselor determines which of three categories and nine total subcategories best matches the person's or family's lifestyle. The adopter receives a colored card and looks for animals with color-matched kennel cards. This approach avoids the overwhelmed feeling that some people get when they see the number of available animals.

Shelter personnel evaluate dogs and cats based on their behavioral traits. For example, a dog with a green color-coded description would be a "Life of the Party," "Go-Getter," or "Free Spirit."

> **Life of the Party.** I think everything is fun, interesting and meant for play, especially you. Anything you do, I'll want to do too. With my own brand of surprises, life with me will keep you constantly on your toes, and the fun is guaranteed. (Socially motivated)[44]
>
> *Copyright © 2011. The American Society for the Prevention of Cruelty to Animals (ASPCA). All Rights Reserved.*

Green dogs love to be both physically and mentally engaged. You can see how such a dog would be a better match for someone who wanted to provide that type of activity rather than someone who wanted a quiet, sedentary companion. The result is a win-win for animals and people.

Shelters: After piloting the program with a number of shelters, Emily and her colleagues learned that organizations had to be ready to embrace change for the program to get the best results. The adopter survey was different from the detailed screening questions that some groups used. If an organization held on to those criteria while adding the Meet Your Match program, fewer animals would come back in, but total adoptions before returns wouldn't grow. In order to allocate the ASPCA's resources to save the most lives, organizations requesting in-person training must not only be of sufficient size to warrant the investment but also demonstrate their willingness to implement the program to its fullest benefit.

I Am Not My Target Audience

You don't think the same way as the people you're trying to change. Listen to them to understand what motivates them.

Emily partnered with shelters to develop models to predict how dogs and cats would behave in the home based on behaviors that could be measured in the shelter. Then she launched pilot efforts to test the models, the program, and the training.

Adopters: These pilots included interviewing people who had adopted under the Meet Your Match program. Questions ranged from whether the animal did act as predicted to how satisfied the adopter was with the experience.

Shelters: I worked with Emily to interview some of the pilot participants to determine what went well and what could have been better in the implementation. With this information in hand, she refined the Meet Your Match program to enhance its ability to meet the needs of adopters and shelters. For example, the data collection process for the Feline-ality assessment created a burden for shelters. Emily was able to streamline the requirements to make the workload more manageable without sacrificing the quality of the assessment.

Education Isn't Enough

It takes more than telling people about a problem to inspire them to act.

Adopters: The Meet Your Match program goes beyond messaging and promotion. It provides important benefits for people to adopt from a shelter rather than go to a pet shop or breeder. The process provides individualized attention to the potential adopter and helps her or him choose an animal more likely to be just the right companion.

Shelters: The training, start-up materials, promotion guides, graphics, talking points, and more that the ASPCA provides deliver a complete system that shelters can implement. That enables them to get up and running as quickly and easily as possible. Training is available by ordering materials, in workshops, and in on-site sessions. The ASPCA does not charge any fee for shelters to use the program.

Voice Matters

How you say it is as important as what you say. Positive change begins with you.
Adopters: The process impresses shelter visitors because of the professional, yet friendly, tone and the focus on adopters. Even the program's "adopter survey" suggests a more collaborative relationship than the common adoption "application." Program materials help shelter personnel use an engaging, conversational approach. The high level of service can generate repeat adopters and word-of-mouth recommendations to others to adopt rather than buy.

Shelters: The ASPCA uses that same professional, yet friendly, tone in communications with shelters, even describing Canine-ality and Feline-ality as, "science-based programs [that] are fun - and highly effective."

Evaluate, Don't Guess

We have to determine if we're getting results and learn from our experience to do better.
The Meet Your Match program provides measurable results, with shelters placing more dogs and cats in homes after they implement it. Participating shelters have achieved gains in adoption often reaching 15% or more. Some organizations have seen 40-60% improvement during times of heavy publicity and promotion.

> **When we tally up the increases in adoptions, decreases in returns, decreases in euthanasia, and decreases in length of stay from shelters who have implemented the program, we are looking at literally tens of thousands of lives saved![45]**
>
> **- Dr. Emily Weiss**

Emily's research during testing for Feline-ality revealed that nearly all Meet Your Match adopters were likely to choose a shelter with the program again. Shelter personnel interviewed during pilot phases, from executive directors to kennel staff, responded enthusiastically about the process.

Shelters can learn more about the Meet Your Match program at http://www.aspcapro. org/aspcas-meet-your-match.php.

If you want to adopt a dog or cat from a shelter using the Meet your Match program, please visit http://www.aspca.org/adoption/meet-your-match/.

Teaching Campus Cafeterias a Thing or Two

Josh Balk always felt hurt when he saw an animal in pain. He knew he wanted to help.

In high school, Josh and some friends watched documentaries about how animals are raised for food. They saw how in industrialized farming, producers reduce costs by keeping more animals in less space and employing any technique that maximizes growth rates. Pigs can't turn around. Egg-laying hens can't spread their wings. Josh wondered how he could love his dog while still supporting the pain and suffering of other animals.

He became vegetarian. In college, he worked with the dining services to add more veg options to the menu. He also made sure the food service personnel packed plant-based items for him and his baseball teammates when they went to away games.

Years later Josh is creating change in colleges and universities around the country and helping activists around the world.

> Something I learned from many of my heroes in the animal protection movement is that I should make strategic decisions as an activist with the end goal being reducing as much animal suffering as possible.[46]
>
> - Interview by Mark Hawthorne, "Josh Balk: Helping Campuses and Companies Reduce Cruelty"

The "Cage-Free Campus" campaign reflects that strategic approach. The idea came as Josh and colleagues at The HSUS considered where to pursue relief for farm animals.

> There are so many issues about farm animals that no campaign could ever reach every one. We wanted to think of an idea that was the best bang for the buck, the greatest reduction in animal suffering… Battery cages are perhaps the most cruel and inhumane practice in agribusiness. [Getting people to switch to cage-free eggs] wouldn't create chicken utopia, but it would make their lives much better.
>
> - Josh Balk

The HSUS's undercover investigation of a factory farm owned by Cal-Maine, the leading U.S. egg producer revealed, "rampant abuse and food safety problems." Cal-Maine has nearly 30 million laying hens and approximately $1 billion in sales.[47]

According to the WSPA, in 2005 over 5.6 billion egg-laying hens were raised worldwide, the majority in battery cages.[48]

> **Up to 90,000 hens can be kept in one shed, in stacks of wire cages so small that the birds cannot walk, stretch their wings, peck and scratch at the ground, or perch. Their bones become so brittle through lack of exercise that many suffer broken bones by the time they are slaughtered.[49]**

- WSPA, *The facts about our food: Intensive poultry farming*

Photo by The Humane Society of the United States[50]

Mahi Klosterhalfen, of Germany, became veg after reading Gandhi's autobiography. He learned about the Cage-Free Campus campaign in podcasts from Erik Marcus, author of books including Meat Market: Animals, Ethics, and Money. Mahi launched the campaign at the university he was attending. Then he spread it to other German universities and into Austria, with support from the Albert Schweitzer Foundation (ASF), where he now holds the position of executive vice president.

Both Josh and Mahi have gotten impressive results with the campaign. Their approach illustrates the elements of the ACHIEVEchange system.

Action and Audience

Our goal is changing behavior. Think of people as customers for change and address their "What's in it for me?"

The campaign goal is to get colleges and universities to switch to cage-free eggs. While there may be potential to add more veg options in the dining hall, the outreach initially focuses on the cage-free issue.

Decision-makers for food service constitute the audience. Their "What's in it for me?" is to successfully run their business operations.

Student activists who work with The HSUS or ASF are partners in affecting change. Partners should be treated like any audience, with their needs considered and addressed. However, this example focuses on the marketing to food service managers.

Create Benefits and Cut Barriers

People take action when they feel the benefits of doing so exceed the barriers.

Dining halls are in the business of making students happy, while managing to budgets. Addressing student demand for more humane alternatives is, therefore, a benefit to dining hall managers, but the increased cost associated with cage-free eggs is a significant barrier.

When he was an undergraduate asking for veg options, Josh didn't understand the practical aspects of running a dining hall. He talked only about animal cruelty. He's realized, however, it would have been more effective to make a complete business case and does so in the Cage-Free Campus campaign. Sustainability, health considerations, and allergy risks can be more compelling benefits, on their own or in combination with animal issues.

Mahi doesn't even need to focus on cruelty. In Germany, people are well aware of battery cages, where laying hens live crammed together with less space than an 8 ½ x 11 sheet of paper. All he has to do is say that dining hall operations are using battery cage eggs.

That doesn't mean that Josh or Mahi gets immediate results. Often they use student petitions to demonstrate the demand for cage-free. Mahi's petitions say that students are willing to pay the additional expense. Getting a small amount more per student (such as $20 per year in the U.S.) can be less of a barrier than a large loss for dining hall operations would be. Some schools reduce expenses elsewhere to pay for the increase.

Five or six years ago, U.S. dining halls couldn't easily source enough cage-free eggs. Therefore, Josh would ask for a phased conversion to make the change doable. Now that the increase in demand has led to sufficient supply, that's no longer a barrier to change.

How to Say Something to Someone Instead of Nothing to Everyone

One size does not fit all. Choose the best people to target and tailor your efforts to them.
Josh and his colleagues carefully chose colleges as an important audience to influence initially. They use a lot of eggs! A single campus might go through hundreds of thousands or even millions each year. Few corporate cafeterias would use as many. By starting with colleges, The HSUS has achieved greater impact.

Students are more likely to be socially conscious and active than typical employees would be. It's easier to mobilize them to press for change. Dining hall managers can't just brush off these requests. They want to avoid confrontation, so may be willing to act when approached.

In the U.S., food service and other campus administrators are often interested to learn that using cage-free eggs can improve their score on The College Sustainability Report Card. They're rarely interested in hearing about which other schools have made the change. Unlike their restaurant counterparts, they don't see themselves in direct competition. Josh therefore tailors the cage-free message differently for colleges and in more recent efforts with restaurants.

I Am Not My Target Audience

You don't think the same way as the people you're trying to change. Listen to them to understand what motivates them.
While The HSUS did not conduct formal research on the needs of dining halls, Josh understands how they work from many years of interacting with them. Mahi studied business at university, so also knows the language and the issues. Being able to talk about food service operations and profitability, along with egg distribution and pricing, increases their credibility.

Josh emphasizes, however, that you don't need to be an expert or study for months to bring the cage-free issue to your school, office cafeteria, or local restaurant. The people he meets with don't often ask many technical questions. They are usually curious about the issue and take it seriously. By listening, he finds out what he needs to address to help them make the switch.

Education Is Not Enough

It takes more than telling people about a problem to inspire them to act.
The dining halls need to know where to get cage-free eggs (*products*). Now that cage-free eggs are more easily sourced (*place* to get them), Josh shares a list of suppliers that have third party audits. This helps the food service operation assure students that the farms are doing what they say. In some situations, Josh offers to introduce the purchasing manager to the suppliers or distributors.

In addition to student fees, other creative approaches can offset the higher *price* of cage-free eggs. At a Massachusetts university, one student suggested a Meatless Monday that would save money to pay for cage-free eggs.

The student wasn't a veg advocate. She was a meat eater with an interest in sustainability issues. *Partnering* with students on campus, including those from a variety of backgrounds who may share an interest in cage-free eggs, is an important part of the campaign's success. Mahi uses Facebook to find potential student partners, but he's also traveled throughout Germany to make connections that are more personal. Those relationships motivate student advocates to persist, even when they don't get immediate results.

The students undertake *promotion* and secure more partners. In addition to circulating petitions, these efforts to galvanize and demonstrate support can include contacting the campus newspaper's editorial board and engaging student government.

Voice Matters

How you say it is as important as what you say.
The Cage-Free Campus outreach is professional and respectful. While the primary goal is to get the dining hall to switch to cage-free, the secondary goal is to create relationships that pave the way for other animal-friendly changes.

> If the requests aren't practical and they [the dining halls] can't meet the demands, no animals will be helped at all. These companies will not think we're going to be a good partner to create humane solutions... What is most effective is to form these relationships so we can continue to do more. Food organizations can always do more. So getting a short-term [win] might help some animals, but probably not as much as if we can build long-term relationships to continue progress as long as possible.
>
> - Josh Balk

Mahi was able to win over an important contact with his positive, professional demeanor. When he called the director of dining for all Austrian universities, the man was initially hostile, saying, "Oh, you're one of those animal rights activists and you want to sabotage my business." Instead of reacting negatively, Mahi remained calm. He explained that he understood that cage-free brings extra costs to food service. He shared that in Germany, universities had been successful asking students to make up the difference. The director agreed to look into cage-free and within three months had found a supplier for all shell eggs and egg products.

Evaluate, Don't Guess

We have to determine if we're getting results and learn from our experience to do better.
Another plus for the Cage-Free Campus campaign is that it produces tangible, measurable results. By 2011, 64% of U.S. universities are using cage-free for at least some of their eggs, according to the Sustainable Endowment Institute. Under Mahi's leadership, two thirds of German universities are cage-free as are all of those in Austria.

Because Josh and Mahi build positive relationships with the dining service directors, cage-free can lead to other animal-friendly changes. The head of dining services for Germany invited Mahi to meet, because he wanted to learn what might be coming after cage-free. Mahi talked about the health, environmental, and cruelty aspects of meat production and asked for more veg options in the university eateries. The director invited him to present at a conference of dining directors from across the country. Many responded positively. Now a vegan chef trains them to offer more plant-based meals. Mahi estimates that about one quarter of the universities have brought in the vegan chef to train their teams.

Want help asking for cage-free options in your campus dining hall, office cafeteria, or local restaurant? Learn more at http://www.humanesociety. org/issues/confinement_farm/facts/cage-free_campus.html. You can even contact Josh for help at jbalk@humanesociety.org or 301-721-6419.

• • • • • • •

Achieve Impact

1. What reactions or ideas did these examples trigger for you?

2. List one or two ways you could improve what you do based on what you've learned.

Chapter 4

Action and Audience

In this chapter:
- To help animals we need to change people's behavior, not just their attitudes.
  - People may change behavior for other reasons and then adopt more animal-friendly attitudes.
- All people ask "What's in it for me?" when we ask them to change.
- Think about the people you want to influence as your "audience for change" rather than "bad people" or "the enemy."
  - You never know when you might be dealing with a future champion for animals!
- Businesses, elected officials, media, and supporters all have their own versions of "What's in it for me?" Learn what they are to increase your effectiveness.

● ● ● ● ● ● ●

We often talk in animal protection about winning hearts and minds. While that's valuable, what we really want is to win hands, feet, and mouths. Our bottom line is action. Changing attitudes isn't enough.

Think about the examples you just considered about avoiding mall and chain store shopping or eating raw food. Maybe you already had an attitude that preserving the environment is important or that people should be treated well in their jobs. What you learned might have even convinced you to think it would be better to change how you shop or eat.

But unless you take action on what you're thinking, it doesn't make any difference. The two examples you read were not effective advocacy if they didn't move you toward changing your behavior.

We see this in our own work all the time. Awareness, knowledge, and attitudes don't reduce animal suffering by themselves. If people know they should get a dog license or microchip but don't do it, we have not been successful. Only action helps animals.

The starting point for effective advocacy is to always focus on how you will ultimately create action.

> ...in order to influence the course of events we knew that we must focus sharply on a single significant injustice, on one clearly limited goal. Moreover, that goal must be achievable.
>
> - Henry Spira[51]

Don't We Need to Change Attitudes First?

Much important work in animal protection addresses attitudes. Changing how people feel about adoptable dogs and cats, fur, circuses with animals, and the conditions under which most farm animals are raised are just a few ways that individual activists and organized campaigns have addressed attitudes to motivate people to act differently.

Changing attitudes isn't easy. Philip Kotler, a leader in both business marketing and social marketing, tells companies, "Because attitudes economize on energy and thought, they can be very difficult to change, and a company is well-advised to fit its product into existing attitudes rather than to try to change attitudes."[52]

If that's the advice for companies with millions and even billions of dollars, it's certainly something to consider for us as individual activists or people working within organizations with budgets that pale in comparison. Where we can link to existing attitudes to motivate action, it makes the job easier. Invoking people's aversion to cruelty is often highly effective. Appealing to other attitudes, such as toward economics or convenience, can sometimes produce better outcomes. That's the bottom-line: behavior change.

Kathy Savesky compares social marketing to dog training regarding the focus on outcomes:

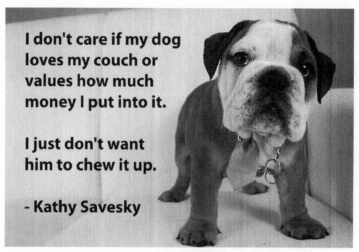

I don't care if my dog loves my couch or values how much money I put into it.

I just don't want him to chew it up.

- Kathy Savesky

Photo by Chris Montiani

Some advocates worry about people who take action for the "wrong" reason. They might say that it's "not good enough" that some people spay or neuter animals because they don't want the hassle of females in heat or males wandering. They may resent those who eat veg food for health reasons. Shouldn't everyone be motivated to help animals?

Well, if any of us were that kitten bound for the euthanasia room or the lamb heading to the slaughter plant, we'd probably be happy for a reprieve for any reason. In addition, *attitudes don't always come before action*. Sometimes people make a change and then align their attitudes to match the behavior. Those of us who've ever bought an item on impulse may have suddenly changed our attitude to justify why the purchase was sensible or even important.

• • • • • • •

A Song Converted Alexis C. Fox

Alexis C. Fox, State Director for Massachusetts for The HSUS, must have become veg for animals reasons, right?

Nope. As a teen, she just thought being a vegetarian was cool! She didn't know anyone who was veg. Some hip song on the radio about a very pretty vegetarian girl motivated her to give it a go.

Then she had to justify her decision to people. That's when she learned about factory farming and started discussing the ethical issues behind meat.

Although Alexis ate fish at first, being vegetarian, and ultimately vegan, became part of her identity. She later started the vegetarian group at Bates College and studied animal law at Lewis & Clark Law School.

The rest, as they say, is history. The animals gained a true supporter just because it was cool to be veg.

• • • • • • •

The Key Question to Inspire Action

When you thought about whether to avoid malls and major retailers or if you would eat all raw food, thoughts raced through your mind about what the impact would be. Where would you go to shop? What would the stores be like? Would you enjoy the food? What happens when you eat out?

Regardless of the specifics, each question was part of your overall evaluation of "What's in it for me?" (WIIFM). We all consider this central question, not necessarily consciously, when we're asked to change. **When you ask someone to do something to help animals, they always think about "What's in it for me?"**

Does WIIFM Mean We're Selfish?

Well it depends how you think about the word. If you define it as considering the world from the perspective of how it affects us then yes, we are selfish.

If by selfish you infer that we're only interested in material things for ourselves, then no, that's too limited a view.

"What's in it for me?" includes how we feel about ourselves and the impact we're having. Altruism – caring about other people, animals, and the environment – can indeed be part of "What's in it for me?" but it's not the only element.

Again, think of your experience with the shopping example. If you believed that shopping at other places (or shopping less) would help the environment, you most likely placed some positive value on that. That may have made you want to do so. However, a host of other factors came into play.

The same happens when we're advocating for animals. When we urge people to do something different, they consider a range of factors to determine "What's in it for me?" To persuade them to adopt new behaviors, we must not only convey what we want them to do but also help them to believe it's in their interest.

Whether it's the person looking at cruelty-free cosmetics, the business evaluating sponsoring a shelter or rescue group event, or an elected official determining whether to support legislation banning puppy mills, each asks "What's in it for me?" Are such people unintelligent or uncaring? Well, certainly you don't view yourself as stupid or callous if you shop at malls and big box retailers or eat cooked foods! And you aren't, of course.

• • • • • • •

Mark Rifkin Answers "What's in It for Me?" to Eat Veg

Veg proponents debate how to motivate people to eat plant-based foods. Promote compassion for animals? ...appeal to health concerns? ...point out the environmental impacts?

Mark Rifkin thinks none of these is the most important issue. After starting with a grassroots group fighting fur, pet stores, the local zoo, circuses, vivisection, and more, he went back for an MS in Health Education to become a registered dietitian. Although he believes in the importance of health and nutrition, of course, Mark knows that people first evaluate taste, convenience, and affordability when choosing what to eat. Research studies confirm the role these factors play.[53]

> **People will eat just about anything if they think it will taste good and if it looks good. If it will lower cholesterol and save money, even better. If it doesn't taste good or look good, they won't eat it.**
>
> - Mark Rifkin

One of the biggest barriers to advancing plant-based eating is that many people don't think veg food will taste good. Mark has made sharing delicious veg food an important part of both his work and his informal outreach. When he runs workshops, he brings vegan dishes that have participants asking for more. He invites friends and colleagues to veg restaurants. He shared the following ideas that anyone can do:

- Have delicious recipes that appeal to non-vegetarians to make for potlucks.
- Take your own food to a dinner or event (ask the hostess or host first) and let others taste it.
- Invite people to eat in your home.
- Give people a gift of food. Make it yourself or buy something from a vegan bakery or natural foods store. As Mark asks, "Who's going to turn down chocolate chip cookies even if they're vegan?"
- Give a gift certificate for a veg restaurant or veg food.

Andrea Sachs of *The Washington Post* also recommended a food-based approach, when reporting on D.C. VegFest:[54]

The way to a carnivore's heart is not through naked celebrities or dewy-eyed bunnies, but through the stomach.

Mark says that people are constantly amazed at how good veg food can taste. While they may not become vegetarian or vegan overnight… or ever, he helps them choose more plant-based foods and save animals.

There are still people who think vegetarians only eat sticks and twigs. Dazzle them with flavor.

• • • • • • •

Sometimes We Have to Change Our Own Attitude First

To be more effective, we need to see the people we're trying to influence as our "audience for change" rather than "the enemy" or "bad people." This shift can be one of the biggest challenges for many advocates. It's also potentially one of the most powerful, however. Focusing less on our anger and more on learning how to persuade people is critical for us to get the best results for animals.

We are committed to a high standard of people care, both internally and externally, because people are the key to meeting our mission…

'People Care' is what it's all about! We are looking for people who like to help people, because if we don't help the people, we can't help the animals

- Dumb Friends League[55]

• • • • • • •

Kelly Peterson Unlocks Attitudes to Unchains Dogs

Kelly Peterson founded Fences for Fido with help from eight girlfriends who wanted to honor a friend who had passed away. Kelly had learned about the Coalition to Unchain Dogs in North Carolina and was excited about launching a similar effort in Oregon.

The group heard about a dog that had been chained for six years. They visited the house and knocked on the door. The family answered. "They thought we were crazy, but they accepted," Kelly says. On a Saturday in May 2009, eight of the women returned with spouses, partners, and friends in tow. Members of Coalition to Unchain Dogs flew cross-country to help. Together they built the fence that freed the dog, Chopper, from his tether.

In just a short time, that small group expanded to 900 volunteers. Fences for Fido had built over 200 enclosures by October 2011 and had a growing waiting list. Kelly attributes much of their success to how they view the people they serve.

> Originally, I thought more about the dog, not the family. As animal people, we find it incomprehensible to think of a dog chained outside. As I've gotten to know the families, the dog is a reflection of the family. They love the dog. They can barely feed themselves, let alone the dog…

> People have guilt about chaining. They don't feel right about it. When you're doing something wrong in your life, you tend to ignore it. They ignore the dog and don't give it attention because they can't afford a fence. Then all of a sudden, they've given this gift to their dog and they have an investment.

> The changes in the family are as touching as the changes in the dog. People say they're a godsend and they've prayed for something like this.

> I could spend time thinking about why the dog is on the chain for five years, but you just have to let that go, and think the best of people.

Fences for Fido turns people with chained dogs into animal advocates. Here's what Chopper's guardian had to say, according to the organization's page on the Care2 website:

> These people are great! They built a fence for my dog for free! I

realize now he is so much happier being off the chain! Never again a chain! Please support them and their cause! They make a huge difference for a dog's life and their owners! I cannot say enough! I am very thankful.

• • • • • • •

Perhaps you can understand chained dogs, but how about lions, tigers, or other wild cats as "pets?" After Terry Thompson's tragic release of exotic animals in Zanesville, Ohio in 2011 and the resulting shooting of most of them, it's hard not to demonize people with exotics. Jeff Kremer of Big Cat Rescue explains that many of them get caught up in ego and money considerations. They don't necessarily have bad intent. Having a big cat gives them something they think they need. It's not about hurting the animal. Some go to great lengths, such as refinishing a basement, to provide what they believe is a good home. That doesn't mean we want the animals to stay in that home, of course. But we can often move toward a better outcome for animals by getting past automatically assuming all such people are conscious evildoers.

Are You Talking with a Future Champion for Animals?

People who are making choices that hurt animals today can become their advocates tomorrow. Someone may engage in only a few animal-friendly activities now, but adopt others later. See if you can match the past behavior on the left with the correct person on the right. The answers appear at the end of this chapter.

Hunted and fished when young	Laura Maloney, Chief of Staff, The HSUS
Spokesperson for the pork industry	Volunteer for Fences for Fido
Was a fur-wearing vegetarian	Andrew Page, Senior Director of the Wildlife Abuse and Fur-Free Campaigns, The HSUS
Hunts bears	Mike King, celebrity advocate to ban sow stalls in New Zealand
Worked in zoos	Caryn Ginsberg, author of **Animal Impact**

Give it a try. There's something that's tremendously liberating when you stop thinking everybody else is the enemy and start understanding where they're coming from. That doesn't mean you're not trying to change them. But give them a break and recognize that they may be motivated by a lot of things.

- Kathy Savesky

Businesses Are People Too

Well, not exactly, although recent U.S. laws are giving them similar rights.

Businesses also have a version of "What's in it for me?" When you approach a business for a sponsorship or donation, to offer reduced fee spaying and neutering, to stop carrying fur, or to use more humane methods to deal with wildlife, they too evaluate your request from self-interest.

Self-interest for a business is usually about money. How will this decision affect the bottom line? Elements that influence profitability include sales, media exposure, expenses, and more. Companies are also becoming more interested in socially responsible ventures that demonstrate they are good citizens.

Although you may think of businesses as faceless entities, you still need a person or group of people to take action. While that person asks what's in it for the business, s/he will also consider personal aspects. Those may include how this decision affects a career, what colleagues will say, and how s/he feels about the issue.

The for-profit world has a lot of heart. However, by appealing purely on heart you won't be as successful as if you look at the business and see what they do and provide something that is a win for them.

We have to remember that businesses have a responsibility to generate returns or profits for shareholders. The win they get may be selling a product. It could also be credit and visibility. Companies are increasingly seeking social engagement and looking for causes that resonate with their customers and employees.

Don't just think about what you are and what you need. Put yourself in the shoes of the person you're talking to and what you can provide them that can be valuable for their business. You have to approach it with a business mindset.

- Sue Della Maddalena, PetSmart Charities

Getting Elected Officials to Vote for Animals

The ultimate goal for office-holders is to be re-elected. What does that take? Think about it and you'll have a big part of the "What's in it for me?"

Did you come up with voter support, money, volunteers, power, and alignment with fellow party members? When you're advancing legislation and seeking sponsors or votes, these are the factors you'll want to consider in addition to appealing to the person's desire to feel good about doing the right thing.

When he was executive director of Humane Society International (HSI), Neil Trent scored a victory for dogs by appealing to an ambitious politician. The mayor of Calama, Chile planned to seek national office. He needed to improve his profile and stand apart from other candidates. Neil suggested implementing a spay/neuter program to address the stray dog problem. He offered to publicize the mayor's effort to raise the humane bar in the community. The recognition HSI gave the mayor on its website and in the press answered "What's in it for me?" for the mayor to support the spay/neuter program.

Joan Dempsey, past director of advocacy for the Massachusetts Society for the Prevention of Cruelty to Animals (MSPCA), listened to legislators in her state to figure out the best way to be effective with them. One of the most important things she learned was that each one has to be a jack-of-all-trades. They need to know a little bit about everything, so they need partners in different issue areas.

Joan and her team built relationships by being dependable partners who provided accurate information on animal issues. Many legislators came to believe that the MSPCA knew animal issues best. They or their staff members then went to the MSPCA when they wanted to find out more about a bill or figure out how to respond to issues that came up in their districts. Meeting the legislators' information needs gave the MSPCA better access and more influence.

Here's Joan's advice if you want to be the go-to source on animal issues in your town or state:

> Become indispensable by being professional, reliable, and non-controversial. You need to understand that doing a sit-in in their office won't get you there.
>
> Ask legislators what they need. We usually go to them when we need something and often forget to ask what we can do to support them.

Ruth Steinberger of SpayFIRST! created a win-win when she asked a state senator to announce grant money she received to start spay/neuter programs in Oklahoma:

> When two funders approved grants, it seemed appropriate to make a press statement. Having articles say that Ruth Steinberger was starting this would mean nothing, as I was a stranger. I called the state senator for that district, a very popular young guy, to see if he wanted to announce it. He immediately said, 'Oh yeah, I love to announce good news, especially with money coming - of course.'

Brenda Shoss, Founder of Kinship Circle, describes how to answer "What's in it for me?" when you're writing letters to legislators or businesses:

> Identify why the reader should consider your point of view.
>
> Begin letters to legislators with 'As a registered voter in your district.' When addressing private industry write, 'As a consumer' or 'As a potential tourist.' If feasible, express your unique link to the issue. For instance, a parent might write: 'As a mother I would like to buy your line of diapers and lotions, but I do not feel confident using items determined safe in animal tests....'
>
> In the concluding paragraph, reidentify yourself: 'My family would be pleased to purchase your products and suggest them to our friends when [the] company switches from outmoded animal tests to tenable non-animal research methods.'[56]

Getting Media Coverage

When you ask a reporter, blogger, or editor to publicize your campaign, program, issue or organization, they too ask "What's in it for me?" Much as we'd like, they aren't there just to bring visibility to animal issues.

The media want to retain and attract readers, viewers, or listeners. Usually that's to support the bottom line because they can sell more advertising, but it may also be in order to gain more impact or prestige, as with a blogger who doesn't use the online platform for income.

To get these results, the media need stories that appeal to current and potential users of their information. That means stories that are interesting and matched to their audiences. To meet the "What's in it for me?" it helps to see what stories have run in the past and what you can learn about the audience. That helps you approach with ideas and information more likely to result in a story.

• • • • • • •

The Straight Scoop on Media from Alexis Raymond

Who better than a former journalist to know what it takes to get media coverage? Alexis Raymond was a journalist and worked in public and media relations in the private sector before serving as communications director at RedRover (previously United Animal Nations) from 2004 to 2011. Here's her firsthand report on what journalists need:

> Journalists are really busy. Nonprofits have this idea, 'Oh, we do great work, it would be great to tell people about it. Why don't you write a story about us and how great we are?'

> But journalism is very specific. Stories are not about broad topics; they're about specific people and specific animals. Journalists want those stories. They want something that's unique and that hasn't been told before.

> So if you can package that story ... if you can say, 'Hey, we have this great story about the animals that were found in an attic during the flood and our people who rescued them, and we tracked down the owner...' if you can give them that story from beginning to end, connect them with the people they need to interview, help arrange the photos, and give them what they need, it's going to make it a lot easier for them and more likely that they will cover it.

> [As animal advocates] we really have to help them put that story together and give them the information that they need as opposed to expecting them to go out and find it.

The more we're willing to do that, the more the media will recognize that we're good people to work with. [Then] journalists will turn to us when they are looking for a story or they want a comment.

• • • • • • •

It also helps to find animal-friendly journalists. According to the ASPCA's ebook *More Hands to Save More Lives*, during the three-month ASPCA Challenge in 2010, Tallahassee-Leon Community Animal Service Center (TLCASC) garnered daily mentions on radio as well as 31 television stories and 15 print stories (the equivalent of $18,000 in advertising). Rather than simply reaching out to the various outlets, they did their homework first, identifying and targeting the animal lovers at newspapers, and TV and radio stations. The organization won the ASPCA Community Engagement Award along with a $25,000 grant. More importantly, TLCASC saved 335 more animals in the August to October period in 2010 than they did in 2009.[57]

Supporters

Even an organization's donors, staff, volunteers, and social media followers ask "What's in it for me?" when choosing how and how much to support your work.

Donors enjoy the satisfaction of being part of what you do. They may also look for results, recognition, prestige, or the opportunity to shape your efforts, among other factors. While this may not seem like rocket science, how well do you know what your current and prospective donors would like? How effective are you in meeting those wishes in order to cultivate more support?

Staff and volunteers want to be part of your cause. They may also want to use their time well, to put their talents to work, to gain new skills, or to meet like-minded people. By thinking more about their "What's in it for me?" you'll be able to help them do their best to do more for animals.

Karen Brown, Director of Programs for RedRover, notes the emphasis that she and her colleagues place on meeting the needs of volunteers for the RedRover Responders program (emergency services).

We put the volunteers first. Volunteers that are better prepared and have a positive experience can enable us to help more animals

better. It's easy to put the animals first and forget that. Our philosophy is that we are here for the volunteers. If we support them right the animals will get what they need.

If you have a Facebook page for your organization, most of your followers are there because they believe in what you're doing. Emily Garman of The Social Animal recommends offering the following content that engages them as active supporters:[58]

- Useful information
- Entertainment
- Sharable content
- Material that makes people feel good
- Easy-to-do actions

Address your audience's "What's in it for me?" in any form of social media using tips like these to move people from interest to action and to attract new followers.

• • • • • • •

Recap

Action and Audience

- Our goal is changing behavior.
- Think of people as customers for change and address their "What's in it for me?"

Achieve Impact

Treating People as an Audience for Change

Think about a business where you enjoy spending your money. It could be an animal supplies store, the local coffee shop, an environmentally friendly drycleaner, an online store, or almost any venture.

1. Consider the WIIFM for you to buy from this business.
   - What does the business do to address your WIIFM?
   - How does the business treat you? What exactly does the business say and do to make you feel welcomed and valued? What don't they say or do?
   - How do you feel about the business? How does that influence your willingness to interact with it again?

2. Now think about a business you once used, but no longer do.
   • What specifically did it do that it no longer met your WIIFM?

3. Compare the difference when a business does and does not meet your WIIFM.

4. What do you do to address WIIFM for the people you're trying to influence? How do they let you know you've met their WIIFM? What are three ways you could do more to meet your audience's WIIFM?

Jot down your thoughts and other key takeaways you got from this chapter.

Don't worry if you don't know yet how to be more effective in addressing people's WIIFMs. We'll look more at that in the chapters ahead.

Answers to "Are You Talking to a Future Champion for Animals?"

Hunted and fished when young	Andrew Page, Senior Director of the Wildlife Abuse and Fur-Free Campaigns, The HSUS
Long-term spokesperson for the pork industry	Mike King, celebrity advocate to ban sow stalls in New Zealand
Was a fur-wearing vegetarian	Caryn Ginsberg, author of **Animal Impact**
Hunts bears	Volunteer for Fences for Fido
Worked in zoos	Laura Maloney, Chief of Staff, The HSUS

Chapter 5

Create Benefits and Cut Barriers

In this chapter:
- People take action when they believe benefits exceed barriers.
  - Make change fun, easy and popular to get the best results.
- Advocacy needs to appeal to emotions, not just provide knowledge.
  - Invoking compassion isn't always the best approach.
  - Beware of using guilt to try to sway people.
  - Evoking emotion doesn't mean being excessively emotional ourselves.
- Decreasing or removing barriers to change is often our biggest challenge.
  - Look for ways to make the animal-friendly action possible, simple, fast, convenient, urgent, and top-of-mind.
- Assess the behavior you're advocating against potential competing behaviors and see if there may be a new option you can share or create rather than just saying, "Don't."

• • • • • • •

You've made changes personally, professionally, or both to help animals. At some level, you asked "What's in it for me?" and found new behavior to be both desirable and possible. The positives of making a difference outweighed any potential negatives.

You probably felt differently about taking action in one or both of our two examples on shopping and eating. When you asked "What's in it for me?" did you see more potential negatives than positives to change?

For example, assuming you found the information on shopping credible you might have found the following reasons compelling to make a change:
- Helping the environment
- Avoiding supporting questionable labor practices
- Not wanting to frequent large corporations

Nevertheless, you may have had concerns about:
- Where else to shop
- Higher prices for organic, labor-friendly goods from specialty retailers
- The quality and selection of secondhand clothing
- The inconvenience of shopping at a thrift shop or consignment outlet

In our raw foods example, maybe you liked the potential for:
- Eating more simply
- Gaining energy
- Helping the environment

However, perhaps you were worried about:
- Whether the food would taste good
- Whether you'd get the nutrients you need
- What you'd do about eating out

When we're considering "What's in it for me?" we focus on what we perceive as *benefits* and *barriers*. A benefit is anything that feels good or positive about taking action. A barrier is anything that seems bad or negative. Sometimes barriers are referred to as costs, but I like barrier because it's something that we as advocates can help remove for people. Cost also implies money, which isn't always the issue.

People Take Action When They Believe Benefits Exceed Barriers

People who already shop exclusively for secondhand clothing or eat mostly raw food may see few or no barriers to doing so. Alternatively, they may be so committed to the benefits that they don't mind dealing with any negatives. However, their opinion doesn't make the barriers any less real or significant to you. Hearing them say "it's easy" or "if you cared about the environment, you'd do it" would be more annoying than convincing.

Sometimes we deny the existence of barriers in our advocacy for animals. We may underestimate how difficult it can be for other people to change. Standing up to teachers requiring animal dissection, saying no to a child begging to see the elephants in the circus, or affording veterinary visits may seem easy to us. Our opinion doesn't make the potential barriers any less real or significant to them, however.

> We're sometimes overwhelmed with the emotion of caring and lose sight that there are real life barriers in place for people. We think compassion for animals should be at the very top of the list, and everyone should do everything right away.
>
> – Alexis C. Fox

People weigh benefits and barriers in personal, professional, and political settings. A woman wants to help by adopting from a local humane society, but worries that shelter animals may have health problems. A business executive is eager to implement more humane practices, but worries that higher-ups will be angry that he or she placed concern for animals above maximizing profits. An elected official favors co-sponsoring a piece of pro-animal legislation, but fears that constituents and supporters will react negatively.

Telling people "Just do it" may work for Nike, but it's not an effective approach for advocates to create change. Unless we tip the scales for people so they feel it's in their interest to take the action we want instead of their preferred alternative, they won't. Our success depends on understanding how people perceive the potential benefits and barriers to change on animal issues. Then we can then use this knowledge to provide solutions, share convincing messages, and motivate action.

Bill Smith ,of Academy for Educational Development, used the terms "**fun, easy, and popular**" to describe what it takes for advocates to motivate new behaviors.[59]

Benefit #1 – "Fun" Means That People Have a Positive Attitude About the Change

The Meet Your Match program, including its catchy name, makes adoption more fun by creating the anticipation of discovering a very special animal. The color-coded passes that adopters receive and the colored kennel cards that shelters display not only make finding the right matches easy but also add a festive air.

Many shelters and rescue groups are using themed adoption events and promotions to make them the go-to for finding a new furry friend. For example, Tallahassee-Leon Community Animal Service Center created a "Reach for the Stars" campaign making shelter animals the stars and enlisting community leaders as "agents" to represent them. Kathy Savesky launched a popular singles night at Peninsula Humane Society to bring in new people and show them that animals provide companionship and facilitate social interaction.

For businesses, governments, and other organizations, "fun" is usually something that appeals to customers or constituents while having a positive economic outcome. For example, when the large number of feral cats in Newburyport, Massachusetts threatened the important tourist trade, Stacy LeBaron and her colleagues at the Merrimack River Feline Rescue Society (MRFRS) offered free adoption services and trap-neuter-return (TNR). The no-cost, humane solution was highly appealing to local government officials, businesses, and residents alike, especially since a previous attempt to trap and kill the cats hadn't solved the problem. MRFRS was able to trap and adopt out many cats to make an immediate improvement. Over time the TNR brought the population under control and ultimately the last member of the cat colony died years later.

Benefit #2 – "Easy" Requires That Advocates Help Remove Perceived Inconveniences or Difficulties in Taking Action

MRFRS provided an easy solution because the organization took care of everything. That doesn't work in every situation, of course. Paying attention to detail and logistics can make it easier for you to get others to activate for animals. For example, if people are willing to add their names to your signature drive, why make them wait? When volunteers were collecting signatures for Proposition 2, the ballot initiative to ban a variety of inhumane farming practices in California, San Diego leader Kath Rogers made sure they had multiple clipboards. This simple step made the process quick for people who wanted to sign and less stressful for volunteers eager to get more names.

You've already read about the importance of making it fast and simple for the media to cover animal issues. Mercy For Animals (MFA) does so by providing special resources journalists can use to communicate about the organization's cruelty investigations. MFA posts a special web page, that's not displayed to the public, with additional film footage, expert statements, a profile of the location in question, a copy of the legal complaint, and other evidence. Reporters can access this information to establish the credibility of the investigation and to get additional detail when developing stories.

PRIORITY VENTURES Group
ACHIEVE IMPACT

1402 N Lincoln St., Suite 211
Arlington, VA 22201-4916
publications@priorityventures.com
703.524.0024

Please PRINT clearly

1, How would you rate your level of satisfaction with this talk? (CIRCLE ONE)

Extremely SATISFIED	Somewhat SATISFIED	Neutral	Somewhat DISSATISFIED	Extremely DISSATISFIED

2. What worked best?

3. What could have been better?

4. Please share one action you will take in your advocacy as a result of this talk.

5. Did you choose to get a copy of *Animal Impact* today? (CIRCLE ONE)   Yes   No
Why or why not?

Thank you!

Remember that your audience determines what's "easy." You might think it's easy to find a specific breed of dog through some combination of area shelters, rescue groups, and online sites, but a prospective adopter may think it's difficult. You might think it's easy to use humane approaches to deal with mice in your home or apartment, but someone else may not.

Benefit #3 – "Popular" Involves Creating a Sense That It's the Norm… Everybody's Doing It

Bring together both veg and non-veg friends at a party, or show photos from a local veg fest, so meat-eating friends see the number and variety of people choosing plant-based foods. Talk about stores that don't carry fur,[60] so people will understand that fewer customers are buying these coats and accessories. Give away or sell shirts, buttons, leashes or other items that say, "I found my new best friend at XYZ Humane," so your community sees how many animals are adopted.[61]

Businesses and governments are as concerned about what other people think as anyone else is:

> Power holders may worry about what their colleagues, friends, and family will think of the action. Provide examples of actions taken by other power holders in similar circumstances to help assure the power holder that she or he is in good company…
>
> Though we may regard [deciding based on] social pressure as a character weakness, if it keeps the power holder from taking responsible action, we need to handle social pressure respectfully yet subtly. Laying out the message in a way that people will find easy to explain, even justify, to others may lift that obstacle.
>
> - Josephine Bellaccomo, Move the Message[62]

When advocating for an anti-confinement bill, Alexis C. Fox tells legislators that major grocery chains, including Wal-Mart, have made their private label eggs cage-free. Eliot Pryor reports that SAFE will urge New Zealand supermarkets to follow the example of Coles, Australia's second largest supermarket chain, by refusing to buy pork from farms that still use sow stalls.

• • • • • • •

Bringing Fun, Easy, and Popular to Laws for Animals

A dog confined to a pen, left with spoiled food, and facing children's taunts drew Belen Brisco into action for animals. Wanting to help the dog while keeping peace with her parents' next-door neighbors, she knocked on their door and asked to take the dog for a walk. With her guidance, by the end of the week the kids were walking the dog and making sure he had fresh food and water.

When she returned home, Belen wanted to advance legislation to prevent chaining and penning. While continuing to help individual animals and their families directly, she volunteered with her local animal services division and got involved with Dogs Deserve Better, an organization that promotes such regulations. She soon teamed up with advocates in neighboring Collier County, Florida to pass a new ordinance. Her hands-on experience working with chaining situations made her a credible spokesperson to the county commissioners.

Belen has since gone on to assist with the adoption of new ordinances in Sarasota and Pembroke Pines. Her work as an independent animal welfare consultant includes traveling to other counties to help implement anti-chaining laws at the request of local residents and/or authorities. She knows how to make change fun, easy and popular for the local governments.

Fun

Belen promotes anti-chaining ordinances as win-win-win. Because dogs left on chains are likely to bark more, neighbors get upset and call animal control. Handling those calls cost the municipality tax dollars. New regulations help residents, government, and animals. Belen also shows how proposed regulations protect the public by sharing research that chained dogs are 2.8 times more likely to bite than unchained dogs. Adam Goldfarb of The HSUS is optimistic about the expansion of anti-tethering ordinances, because officials appreciate the opportunity to address both the humane treatment of animals and community safety at the same time.[63]

Easy

Getting conceptual agreement is one thing, but crafting the wording requires more time and attention. Belen works with other advocates, animal services personnel, and other local government officials to create a draft that minimizes enforcement headaches. For example, some people propose allowing chaining for a limited amount of time. But how can officers easily track how long an animal has been tied up outside? Belen speeds this part of the process by sharing ordinances from other communities as models. The HSUS also shares sample in its guide, *A Dog's Life: Chaining and Your Community*.[64]

Popular

Showing what works in other counties gets local leaders on board early in the process. When approaching the Sarasota County board about an ordinance, she included the Collier County ordinance in her initial contact. With each county that passes new regulations, anti-chaining becomes the norm in Florida.

• • • • • • •

Benefits and Barriers Are Ultimately Emotional

> Knowing something isn't enough to cause change. Make people feel something.
>
> – Chip Heath and Dan Heath, <u>Switch: How to Change Things When Change Is Hard</u>[65]

People act based on how they feel, not just what they think. They don't buy a car with a 280 horsepower engine because they're excited about the size and shape of the metal under the hood. Instead, they value the emotional benefits the engine delivers: confidence in better acceleration for safety, the comfort of a smoother ride, or the pleasure of driving faster. Car manufacturers appeal to these emotions in their ads. You've probably seen stunt drivers operating at high speeds and taking improbable turns in unlikely locations. The average driver will never replicate these scenarios, but it creates enjoyable fantasies and impressions of what owning the car would be like. That inspires some people to feel happy about buying the model advertised. It's all about making people happy.

Companies sometimes show their products delivering benefits by relieving negative emotions. Commercials for alarm systems reduce the homeowner's fear of a burglary. Mouthwashes and mints say they'll help you avoid the embarrassment of bad breath. Many nonprofit campaigns also seek to stop certain behaviors by linking them to negative emotions. For example, making smoking seem uncool creates negative emotion about the habit. The intended result is that people will then feel better about giving up cigarettes or never starting with them.

Animal advocates often appeal to people's feelings of compassion. That's not always the best emotion to try to rouse, however.

For example, in 1996 Massachusetts voters passed a ballot initiative to ban certain types of wildlife traps. Each year thereafter the trapping lobby reintroduced bills to overturn the ban. When Scott Giacoppo was deputy director at the MSPCA, his job included fighting these bills.

Rather than frame the debate on cruelty, he tapped people's anger at potential misuse of the legislative process. The vote reflected the will of the people of Massachusetts. Why would lawmakers allow a small special-interest group to overturn the will of the electorate?

Scott found that this message was more effective than the traditional approach urging the compassionate treatment of beavers. He was able to fend off ongoing challenges to the ballot initiative.

Creating a heartfelt response doesn't mean being sentimental in our approach. Conveying too much of our own emotions is risky. Our commitment to helping animals often impresses or inspires people. Excessively vociferous or teary protestations, however, can take the focus off the issue and on to our credibility.

• • • • • • •

Making Businesses Feel Good About Helping Animals

Philip Lymbery became an avid birdwatcher at age 12. He marveled at the wonders of flight and migration. He was, therefore, shocked when a presenter at his school showed how hens in battery cages could not even spread their wings. He has worked to help these birds ever since, currently as chief executive of Compassion in World Farming (CIWF) in Surrey, England.

After using primarily pressure tactics to create change in the 1990s, Philip and his team have shifted to more positive approaches for the last decade. The Good Egg Award is an upbeat idea that's had impressive results. The award recognizes companies that use only cage-free eggs or have made the commitment to do so.

> Instead of shouting at companies, we started to ring them up. We told them switching to cage-free would be great for their companies. They could win an award that would be good for their brand reputation, good for staff morale, and good for animals. Who wouldn't want that?

The Good Egg Award delivers many objective benefits that would make sense to the most hard-nosed business analyst. But even corporate leaders and employees are motivated by emotions. The award can bring recognition, improved image, and improved morale to a company. Those results make executives *feel happy* about going cage-free, maybe even *more secure* in their jobs. Technical assistance provides knowledge and resources to make the switch. That allows personnel to *feel confident* about succeeding. By earning an award, they *don't have to worry* about lagging behind competitors that have already received recognition.

> Never underestimate the power of peer pressure. We hold prestigious events celebrating award winners. One major company attending had only been convinced to try cage-free on trial. At the end of the evening, representatives made the company's commitment permanent.

The Good Egg Award has liberated 25 million hens from cages. Spread wing to wing, that number would stretch half way around the globe. Philip's team works across the European Union, including with Mahi Klosterhalfen in Germany. The RSPCA Australia and the Royal New Zealand Society for the Prevention of Cruelty to Animals have taken on the program as well. CIWF has also added Good Chicken, Good Dairy, and Good Pig designations to its Good Farm Animal Welfare Awards.

• • • • • • •

Pursuing positive outreach doesn't mean abandoning pressure tactics when needed. If a company doesn't respond, it can be appropriate and valuable to urge advocates and the public to make their displeasure known, hold demonstrations, and call out the business in the media. When these efforts detract from a company's image, cause them to lose customers, or overwhelm personnel handling calls, emails, and social media comments, they increase the benefits for decision-makers to take the animal-friendly action and stop the negative impact.

Guilt Is Usually a Barrier to Change

Appealing to negative emotions can be highly effective. The question is which emotions you can tap and how much.

Animal advocacy campaigns often create guilt around one behavior in order to promote the opposite. However, in his book <u>Change of Heart</u>, Nick Cooney, of The Humane League, states, "The research is crystal clear... that using guilt in advertisements and materials is not persuasive... The only relevant exception to this is a situation where people notice their own hypocrisy on a particular issue without it being pointed out to them."

Maura Mitchell of Brandology reported the following regarding guilt and environmental behavior:

> It's counterintuitive, but educating a consumer about their environmental footprint makes it less likely they will engage in green behavior. That's the intriguing conclusion of recent research from The University of Santa Clara, and it's backed by several other studies as well.
>
> When told their personal impact on the planet, the average consumer feels guilty, becomes overwhelmed, and subconsciously aligns their beliefs with their current actions, rather than vice versa.
>
> ... consumers' first response to green guilt is to try to forget the information that made them feel guilty, not to make changes.[66]

People don't want to think of themselves as villains. They are likely to reject approaches that make them feel threatened. So telling them directly that they're irresponsible about their dog or cat, or even implying it by saying "if you were responsible, you would..." isn't likely to succeed. Now you can also understand why people don't want to look at photos of factory farming or other animal exploitation. If they suspect they'll need to make a massive behavior shift, they'll feel overwhelmed and not want to take in information that contradicts their beliefs that everything's okay.

Karly Gould, who runs the RedRover Readers program, points out that even children will recognize and resist guilt appeals.

> If a child has a chained dog in the yard, he or she will align with the family. We need to provide a safe environment, so that child

doesn't withdraw. By hearing the other students discuss the issue, the child can reflect on the dog's situation.

RedRover's nonjudgmental approach gets results. For example, one teacher reported that a child whose family engages in dogfighting began "thinking about it in a different way instead of accepting it as what should happen." That child began asking the parents why they would participate in dogfighting.[67]

We can and should share the ways in which animals suffer…. but with care. We need to help people surface their own concerns. Then give them ways they can be part of the solution, ways they see as manageable, preferably as fun, easy and popular.

Remove Barriers to Change

Surveys show that the overwhelming majority of the public is opposed to cruelty. Our biggest challenge is often, therefore, to help remove the barriers people see to acting on that sentiment.

In his book <u>Marketing Social Change</u>, Alan Andreasen describes barriers to action and ways to overcome them.[68] You can use this summary framework to identify ways to reduce barriers to animal-friendly actions:

If people feel the action is...	Make it...	How?
Impossible	**Possible**	Look at factors you can control to create a new solution, reduce the cost, or make the action seem more doable.
Complex	**Simple**	Streamline the desired behavior or create a step-by-step commitment.
Time consuming	**Fast, Convenient**	Simplify the desired behavior, make it more accessible, or bring it to a closer location.
Low priority	**Urgent**	Repeat calls to act now, and/or get immediate commitments.
Forgotten	**Top-of-Mind**	Provide cues and reminders, preferably at places where people can take action.

The first three barriers – impossible, complex, and time-consuming – usually require modifying what we're asking or changing what it takes to act. If eating vegetarian or vegan sounds impossible, Meatless Monday makes getting started possible. If researching companies that don't test on animals is complex, the Leaping Bunny logo makes it simple for consumers. If taking an animal to a distant spay/neuter clinic is time consuming, mobile units can make the procedure fast and convenient.

Reducing these barriers makes it easier to tip the benefits and barriers scale in favor of action. The last two barriers, low priority and forgotten, are both forms of inertia. People may not be opposed to acting, but it's just not high on their seemingly never-ending to-do lists. While animals rate very highly for advocates, for most people jobs, finances, family, illness, other social issues, and more can move humane actions farther down.

• • • • • • •

Adele Douglass Helps People Vote with Their Wallets

Adele Douglass's mother taught her that all living things have feelings. She encouraged her to listen to and learn from diverse individuals.

After working for a congressman, including managing animal welfare issues, Adele became director of American Humane Association's (AHA) Washington, D.C. office. There she advanced a legislative agenda to protect children and animals.

She also became involved in a project about hog farming. She was horrified to discover how industrial farming operations treat animals. After visiting UK farms using more humane practices and learning about the success of the RSPCA's Freedom Food program, she envisioned a similar program for the U.S. to let consumers vote with their wallets for food producers to treat animals better.

Adele initially created the Free Farmed® program for AHA. Later she cashed in her pension and worked 18-hour days from her apartment to launch the Certified Humane Raised & Handled® program. I worked with her to establish and refine the marketing strategy.

The program reduces barriers for people to purchase products from animals raised to higher care standards by making it:

Possible Before Adele's efforts, there was no way for shoppers to differentiate products in the grocery store based on how producers treat animals.

Simple Shoppers now only need to look for the Certified Humane label.

Quick, convenient Getting into more grocers and restaurants has been a central part of Adele's strategy to making purchase quick and convenient.

Urgent *USAToday, Consumer Reports, Mother Jones, Good Housekeeping*, and *Time* are just a few of the outlets that have publicized the program.

Top-of-Mind People see the label at the point of sale, right as they are making their decision. There are promotional materials in some grocers as well.

The program also addressed barriers for farmers who wanted to treat animals more humanely:

I learned that the issue for farmers was the cost of raising animals differently… if consumers were willing to pay for it, they would make the changes required. They, too, felt trapped by the system. I realized the solution for both farmers and animals was the market.

Each farm undergoes inspection initially and annually thereafter. Even though these farms provide care that already ranks them in the upper echelon, each has made improvements for animals because of these inspections.

The program covered more than 32 million animals as of 2011. In 2006, Adele received the ASPCA's Lifetime Achievement Award.

• • • • • • •

Consider Benefits and Barriers for Competing Behaviors

People evaluate benefits and barriers based on their thoughts about competing behaviors. As the name implies, competing behaviors are alternative actions that your audience can take. Often there will be multiple alternatives to consider, such as:

- Adopt from a shelter, visit a pet store, go to a breeder, get an animal in the want ads, adopt from friends or family, or take in an animal off the street
- Buy a fur coat, get a coat with fur trim, buy a faux fur coat, buy something else
- Go to a circus with animals, go to a circus without animals, engage in another form of entertainment
- Use animals for experiments, use computer simulations, review existing research, don't conduct any research at all
- Sponsor animal-friendly legislation, vote for it but don't sponsor, vote against it, offer a modification

Competing behaviors can influence how people view the benefits and barriers for the behavior you're promoting. Someone only considering purchasing an animal from a pet store or breeder might see the lower cost at a shelter as a benefit. Someone else looking at a "free to a good home" ad would see that same cost as a barrier. So when looking at the benefits and barriers for the behavior you're advocating, consider what the competing behaviors are and how the behavior you want compares.

Often animal advocacy comes across as either/or, yes/no choices where we're saying, "Don't" - don't go to the circus with animals, don't wear fur, don't eat meat. Adults don't like hearing "no" any more than the average two-year-old, however. We may not respond much better either.

> **Loss equals pain for most of us. If we feel like we're losing something or giving something up... it's going to be painful.**
>
> **- Anthony Robbins,** *Personal Power II: The Driving Force*

We can help animals by creatively coming up with new competing behaviors or making our audience aware of ones they may not have considered, rather than just saying, "No."

• • • • • • •

Creating a Win-Win for Birds and People

The Arlington, Virginia-based organization Rare trains community-based conservation leaders around the world how to use social marketing to change human behaviors that harm the environment and wildlife. The organization partnered with the Manomet Center for Conservation and with local Argentinean groups to protect the winter habitat of the Red Knot. This colorful, medium-sized sandpiper flies more than 8,000 miles each spring from as far south as Tierra del Fuego to its breeding grounds in the Arctic Tundra.[69]

The San Antonio Bay Natural Protected Area in Rio Negro, Argentina, is the single most important stopover in South America. Red Knots feast there before their long northward journey. Many stop on the beaches of Las Grutas, a popular vacation destination during Argentina's summer. Beach visitors, especially 4X4 vehicle riders, were disturbing the birds' feeding, nesting, and resting.

Rare's campaign achieved greater enforcement of existing laws prohibiting destructive activity on the beach and raised awareness of fines. To reach the team's goal of reducing disturbances of the birds by 60%, however, public engagement was critical.

Simply telling 4x4 riders to stay off the beach would create a win-lose. Birds gain, riders lose. The team instead worked with the municipal government to build a trail in one area, giving riders a legal place to take the 4x4s while limiting impact to that area only.

By moving from a "just say no" approach to creating a competing behavior to use the legal trail, the team removed a key barrier to change. Initial estimates for 2010 indicated an increase in the number of Red Knots using the beach.

• • • • • • •

Other examples of creating competing behaviors that help animals include:

√ Designing and promoting alternatives to dissection

> ...in 2008, the National Science Teachers Association amended its position statement to reflect the effectiveness of non-animal learning methods and to encourage their use.[70]

> – PETA

√ Offering design students faux fur

> **When students see that they can get the same look and feel of animal fur without the cruelty, the obvious choice is to leave animal fur off their designs.**[71]
>
> - Andrew Page, The HSUS

√ Developing a pigeon contraceptive as an alternative to lethal methods for controlling pigeon populations

> **It's totally humane, totally safe -- you can reverse it if you've gone too far... It doesn't do any good to shoot 'em or kill 'em because they'll just breed back in.**[72]
>
> – Civic association president quoted by *AOLNews* regarding success of OvoControl P from Innolytics

• • • • • • •

Recap

Action and Audience
- Our goal is changing behavior.
- Think of people as customers for change and address their "What's in it for me?"

Create Benefits and Cut Barriers
- People change when they perceive the benefits of doing so to exceed the barriers.

Achieve Impact

1. Consider one or both of the examples on shopping or eating. How could an advocate for the recommended behavior make it...
   - Fun
   - Easy and
   - Popular

   ...to make it more likely that you would take action?

2. Choose one animal-friendly behavior that you advocate. What ideas do you have on how you could make it more fun, easy, and popular for the people you're trying to influence?

Chapter 6

How to Say Something to Someone Instead of Nothing to Everyone

In this chapter:
- A more targeted approach can get much better results than one size fits all.
  - One-on-one interactions provide an excellent opportunity to tailor what you say to the needs of the person you're addressing.
- When talking to many people at once, define groups who have similar needs, attitudes, and behaviors based on…
  - Who are they?
  - How do they think?
  - Where is the problem most or least severe?
  - What's their stage of decision-making?
- People usually move from awareness to interest to decision to action to maintenance on a new behavior.
  - Focus on maintenance so that hard-won gains aren't lost. This issue is especially important for veg advocates.
  - Targeting people closest to action and helping them remove barriers can get more people on board.
  - As people move along the spectrum, they become more concerned about perceived barriers to change.
  - Creating awareness is critical, but it's not enough.
- There is no one right way to define your target. Consider all four questions, especially regarding stage of change, and look for opportunities to combine elements to get the best results.

• • • • • • •

Have you ever tried on a shirt or dress labeled "One Size Fits All?"

Did it fit? Probably not. How could the same garment be appropriate for people who come in all sizes and shapes?

The manufacturer should be honest and label it "One Size Fits Some." It doesn't fit all.

One size does not fit all.

Copyright LifeonWhite.com

The same goes for effective advocacy. One size does not fit all.

To see why, think back to our example about avoiding shopping at the mall and national chain stores. You'll recall that the main message was about how the production process for much new clothing can harm laborers and the environment.

Imagine that an advocate was trying to persuade the following three women to shop secondhand as an alternative:

- Jana sees herself as a creative. Mass-produced items aren't for her. She loves all things retro.
- Andrea is a bargain hunter. She enjoys finding the best deal and sees shopping as recreation.
- Sarah helped start the organic farm at her university, because she's very concerned about how pesticides affect health and the planet.

Do you think the discussion about the environment and human rights would work equally well with each of these women? Why or why not? Would you say something different to any of them?

While we don't have a complete understanding of these women, from what we know…

- The "do good" message might appeal to Sarah more than the others.
- Jana might like that she could put together unique outfits including vintage items at thrift shops or consignment stores.
- The prospect of saving money could be a draw for Andrea.

A more targeted approach can get much better results than one size fits all.

A Big Advantage for Individual Activists!

If you're talking one-on-one, you have the perfect opportunity to tailor what you say to engage people on what's in it for them. While you may have general ideas about what will be persuasive, you can change it up based on how someone responds. Listen to people's reaction to benefits and barriers. Then focus on the ones that are most compelling. This is one of the reasons that personal outreach can be so powerful!

Succeeding at One-to-Many

What if you're working on a campaign, program, or other outreach effort to inspire many people at once? The key is to choose a group of people likely to respond to a similar approach, but one that's different from how others would respond. Then design your efforts to address that group, rather than trying to reach everyone at once. For example, you might promote humane wildlife services in different ways to homeowners who make their own decisions compared to apartment dwellers who would work with building management. A small organization or even a large one just starting work in this area could choose one group as its focus.

This may seem counterintuitive. Don't we want everyone to take every animal-friendly action? Maybe, but remember how limited our resources are compared to the magnitude of the problems and the opposition. One hundred percent results aren't likely any time soon. Treating everyone the same way will slow our progress.

Fortunately, motivating a small number of people to act can actually create momentum that leads to more coming on board. In The Tipping Point, Malcolm Gladwell explains that, "…ideas and behavior and messages and products sometimes behave just like outbreaks of infectious disease."[73] After they reach a critical mass, they suddenly take off.

To understand why targeting a subset rather than everyone makes sense, return to our one-size-fits-all example. Imagine that you're a storeowner with one hundred dresses, ladies size 12. The women who've signed up for your mailing list have indicated whether they're looking for small, medium, large, or extra large sizes.

Would you send a direct mail campaign about the dress to all of them? If you did, you'd probably waste a lot of money promoting to women unlikely to buy. Worse, you might anger customers who thought you were wasting their time. If a size 12 corresponds to a medium, you'd capture most of the potential sales while saving money, by sharing the message with the women who'd indicated they want that size. When customers came in, you'd show the dress to those who looked like the dress would fit. Engaging women who were much smaller or larger wouldn't be a very good use of time. You'd be better helping them find something else.

The Best Approach Is a Targeted Approach

I don't know the key to success, but the key to failure is trying to please everybody.

- Variously attributed to Bill Cosby and others

Defining different groups based on needs and approaching them differently is called **segmentation**. Don't worry about the terminology, though. The concept is as simple as in our dress example. Match what you offer to subsets of people based on their needs, attitudes, and behaviors. When you choose not to go after everyone, but instead pick one group or some groups to pursue, that's called **targeting.**

Some activists resist segmentation and targeting, because it doesn't seem "fair" or "egalitarian." Remember that targeting isn't discrimination. It doesn't mean that you like some people more or think some people are better than others. Rather it is a way to invest your limited resources to produce better results for animals.

Say you set up a table at an event geared to low-income individuals to talk about your spay/neuter clinic. If someone stopped by who seemed to be wealthy, you wouldn't just send her away, thinking "She's not in my target audience, so I won't talk to her." Instead, you'd ask if she'd had her animals altered. If not, rather than offer her one of your clinic's subsidized surgeries, you'd recommend she speak with her veterinarian.

Even when you target one group, you may influence another. My design on the next page for a grocery store handout appeals especially to mothers of young families because of the image of the little girl.

BECAUSE YOU
CARE
ABOUT THE
FOOD
YOU EAT

LOOK FOR THE LABEL

Make absolutely sure the egg, dairy, meat or poultry products you buy were raised right: humanely and without a diet of antibiotics or hormones.

CERTIFIED HUMANE
RAISED & HANDLED

www.CertifiedHumane.org

* Meets the Humane Farm Animal Care Program standards, which include nutritious diet without antibiotics, or hormones, animals raised with shelter, resting areas, sufficient space and the ability to engage in natural behaviors

Copyright Humane Farm Animal Care

Although the card targets moms, anyone interested in the how they eat and/or how farmers and ranchers treat animals could decide to purchase Certified Humane products rather than factory-farmed alternatives after seeing the card.

There are many different ways to define your targets to influence the public, businesses, organizations, or governments to change.

1. Who Are They?

General, objective factors, called demographics, include gender, age, income, primary language, animals in the home, and many other characteristics. Here are just a few examples of using descriptive information to define and choose whom to target.

Targeting by Age

Compassion Over Killing launched pro-veg ads on MTV to reach teens and young adults. Research showed that younger people are more receptive to the compassion message. Articles and reports revealed that this audience is interested in new information about what's really happening in the world. The COK team created its campaign, "A Side of Truth." One ad shows a young woman ordering at the drive-thru of a fast-food restaurant. The voice through the speaker box repeats back her order, but with a twist, "Meat from a pig who can't even turn around, an egg from a bird kept in a cage so small she can't spread her wings, and the milk of a cow whose calf is taken at birth to make veal." The spot ends showing "TryVeg.com."

Sample feedback shared on the COK website shows that the side of truth theme resonates:

> Every time I eat, I think about those images of animals, even though I haven't touched any meat since that night ... How is it possible that I never knew about this? All these years I had no idea that such disgusting abuse was going on. Your ad was such an eye opener, and I just wanted to say thank you.

COK, founded by young people and with "Compassion" in its name, made a good decision to concentrate resources by targeting its campaign to teens and young adults, rather than trying to do too many things at once.

> As a small organization with limited resources, COK strives to work as cost-effectively and strategically as possibly—and several of our national campaigns demonstrate that you don't need a lot of money to bring about positive and meaningful changes for animals.... our MTV Pro-Vegetarian Commercial campaign... has proven to be incredibly cost-effective and successful... Overall, our ads have been viewed over 25 million times nationwide at less than a penny per view—and the feedback from viewers has been phenomenal.[74]
>
> - Erica Meier, COK

Does this mean that every organization and individual should use only the compassion message? Research suggests otherwise. A Humane Research Council study from 2005 showed that vegetarians and vegans combined constituted 1% of U.S. adults. (Other surveys have measured 3%-5%, but some variability in results is inherent in measuring a small percent of the population.) They were more likely to be under 35 and driven by compassion messages. HRC also identified a segment it termed "Meat Reducers," people who reported eating less meat than a year ago. This group represented 26% of adults. Over 60% of them were aged 45 and older, with a disproportionate share aged 65 and above. This group was more likely to cite health factors.[75]

> **Older people are more concerned about health. A 16 year-old boy doesn't even know he has a prostate. But a 76 year-old man is thinking about cancer.**
>
> **- Neal Barnard, Physicians Committee for Responsible Medicine**

Of course, there are young people interested in plant-based foods for health reasons and older people motivated by compassion. In general, however, veg advocates can do as COK has done and match one message to one demographic. Other research by HRC showed that combining compassion, health, and environment messages in a single appeal was less effective than using one reason. Telling everybody everything isn't the answer.

> **Health-related issues topped the list.... This suggests that vegetarian advocates must also be multifaceted in their approaches by using different messages with different audiences, ...It is essential for advocates to recognize that a single message will not work for all audiences. It is paramount that veg*an [vegetarian and vegan] advocates target the right messages to the right audience.[76]**
>
> **- HRC,** *Advocating Meat Reduction and Vegetarianism to Adults in the U.S.*

Would recommending different actions, not just reasons, to older and younger audiences get better results? Veg advocates might save more animals' lives by asking people age 45+ to increase plant-based foods in their diet rather than presenting being a vegetarian (or vegan) as the only desirable outcome. The current and potential meat reduction segment is bigger than the now-veg and likely-to-become veg group. Something less than 100% will be more "fun, easy, and popular" for most people, especially those who see "vegetarian" as labeling them part of a lifestyle or world view they don't share. If five people eliminate five meat meals a week, that's more meat-free meals than if someone eating meat at every meal goes all veg.

This idea is controversial. Are organizations that promote "reduce," "replace," etc. really committed to achieving a vegan world? Will we miss the opportunity to move cultural views, not just for animals used for food but for all animals? Do people only see health and weight improvements that keep them motivated if they go all vegetarian or vegan? Is it too easy to backslide without an absolute standard? (More on backsliding vegetarians later.)

It comes back to action, benefits and barriers, and targeting. The behavior is for people to eat fewer animal-based products. With some groups of people, an all veg strategy might not be the best way to achieve that. One study of meat consumption across countries suggests that a multi-pronged approach, rather than one-size-fits-all, is working:

> **With health, sustainability, religious and animal welfare issues giving meat a bad name and driving up prices, Western consumers are cutting back on their meat consumption, either by fully embracing vegetarianism/veganism or by adopting a pescetarian, "flexitarian" or vegetable-oriented diet.**
>
> **- Euromonitor International**[77]

When HRC points out that "vegetarian advocates must also be multifaceted in their approaches by using different messages with different audiences," that means collectively. It doesn't mean that any person or organization must use vegan, vegetarian, and meat reduction calls to action. Instead, we can each consider how to be most effective, while appreciating that those who work on different parts of the plant-based foods spectrum may be strengthening rather than detracting from a shared goal of saving lives and reducing suffering.

Targeting Decision-Makers

Stephanie Downs has negotiated with numerous businesses on behalf of PETA. She recommends being proactive and targeting the right individual when you're trying to drive change at a company where you work or at any organization.

> **The key is to find out who within the company has the power over the decision.**

For example, if a mid-size to large company is sponsoring rodeo, the head of marketing is the place to start. If you want a business to stop using glue traps, the director of operations makes that call. In a small venture, the owner or president calls all the shots.

Targeting Elected Officials by Their Base

You might approach elected officials differently based on the regions they represent or the types of employment in their state. Representatives of states with little hunting and fishing, for example, are more likely to sponsor and vote for proposed regulations than their colleagues from states where these are major activities. Politicians with industrial agriculture operations in their districts are not going to be the best place to start gathering supporters for your anti-factory farming bill.

2. How Do They Think?

Objective factors don't tell the whole story. Does everyone who's the same gender, age, and income level as you think the same way you do? Targeting people based on their overall outlook or their opinion on your issue can be highly effective.

You can get impressions of how people think from where they live, what car they drive, what clubs or groups they belong to, and how they spend their time. For example, members of a rabbit enthusiast's club might be more concerned about product testing. You won't be right for every individual when inferring attitudes, but you'll get some useful ideas. In the next chapter, we'll cover how to get more and better information.

• • • • • • •

Targeting a Nontraditional Audience by Reframing Vivisection

Anthony Bellotti has been involved in animal protection for over 15 years as a consultant, a volunteer, and a founding board member of the Humane Research Council. He launched the White Coat Waste Project to appeal to the conservative community's distaste for wasteful government spending.

While examining the U.S.'s 2010 economic stimulus package, Anthony came across a curious use of taxpayer money: The Wake Forest University Baptist Medical Center was awarded $71,623 to study the effects of cocaine on monkeys. The story quickly made inroads in the conservative blogosphere.

Republican Senators John McCain and Tom Coburn placed it on their list of the 100 worst stimulus projects.

> **I had an epiphany: it might be possible to reach Republicans and conservatives, a major, yet under-represented audience, by reframing the anti-vivisection debate on fresh, pro-taxpayer terms.**

By highlighting needless government spending on experiments such as studying drug-addicted monkeys, Anthony will capitalize on existing attitudes against wasting tax money.

It's too soon to report results for the White Coat Waste Project. We can see, though, how Anthony's creative idea taps existing attitudes to motivate people who might not respond to typical compassion messages. Matthew Scully's focus on the Biblical concept of stewardship in his book Dominion is also an example of targeting conservatives with messaging designed to appeal to them.

• • • • • • •

Political views and affiliations are especially useful to appeal to elected officials. You can also review individual voting records, committee assignments, and websites to learn more about where they're coming from and how you might engage them. For legislation, sponsors and co-sponsors usually come from the ranks of the more animal-friendly officials. The swing votes you need to pass the bill may be neutral or even negative, requiring a different approach.

A business's strategy reflects the thinking of the management team. Andrew Page of The HSUS considers differences between companies carefully when working with them on fur. For retailers that have only some items with fur trim, he may be able to persuade executives to drop fur entirely. That's not likely for luxury retailers that have high profile fur salons. In those cases, getting the company to stop selling raccoon dog fur or karakul lamb coats can reduce animal suffering now, where pressing for elimination immediately wouldn't get any results. Removing fur from luxury retailers, indeed all retailers, remains the ultimate goal.

3. Where Is the Problem Most or Least Severe?

Targeting where a problem is most common or biggest can help more animals.

• • • • • • •

Go Where the Problem Is

Kathy Savesky began her career in animal protection as a shelter volunteer. Many years later as executive director of Peninsula Humane Society (PHS) in northern California, she learned about social marketing when a volunteer brought in a copy of Alan Andreasen's book <u>Marketing Social Change.</u>

Kathy integrated social marketing into the organization's strategic planning. Although its spay/neuter clinic had been open for 20 years, high levels of intake (the number of animals entering the shelter) and euthanasia persisted.

In analyzing PHS's data, Kathy saw that more cats came in than dogs. Although the number of puppies was small, 65% of them came from geographic areas representing less than 10% of the human population of PHS's service area.

Kathy began by reallocating some of the clinic slots to cat surgeries. She increased the number of feral cat procedures by partnering with local feral cat groups, an uncommon collaboration at the time. Results showed that each feral spay or neuter led to an almost immediate decrease in the number of cats euthanized.

PHS also targeted the areas generating the disproportionate share of puppies. The staff worked with community centers and churches to invite people to vaccination clinics. Youth groups went door to door with fliers. On event days, PHS personnel talked with people waiting in line, offering free spay/neuter if they would sign up for an appointment. Workers were fluent in whatever language predominated in the area and shared translated materials.

Esther Mechler, Founder of Spay/USA, highlighted Kathy's targeted approach in Best Friends' *No More Homeless Pets Forum*:

> One of the many things I learned from Kathy Savesky ... is the importance of segmenting your market.... One of the pieces of information we do have about the cat/dog surplus is that a disproportionate number of breeding animals come from poverty areas. These are the main areas we need to target.[78]

The ASPCA has a Geographic Information System (GIS) that can help shelters make their targeting more precise. The GIS can show intake on a map and then overlay where animals live that have been spayed or neutered. This creates a picture of how well surgeries are reaching neighborhoods with dog and cat overpopulation problems. The system even supports mapping by breed to allow decision-makers to understand at-risk populations, such as pit bulls. Shelter leaders can then deploy resources to where they can do the most to save lives.

• • • • • • •

Sometimes rather than targeting where the problem is biggest, going after a smaller opportunity may increase the likelihood of winning and/or may achieve gains more quickly.

New Zealand's SAFE has spent 20 years working to improve the welfare of chickens. Although public awareness has increased and the free-range egg industry has grown, there hasn't been a quick victory. The powerful, well-organized chicken trade has been too much to overcome. SAFE's efforts continue to move the issue forward. Polls show between 75% and 80% of New Zealanders oppose keeping hens in cages.[79] The Green Party and a candidate from the ACT party have pledged to oppose cages.[80] Together these parties represented just over 10% of the votes cast in 2008.[81]

SAFE got quicker results when taking on the somewhat smaller pork industry. The goal was to eliminate sow stalls, which a minority of farmers used. When a well-known comedian who'd been the spokesperson for the pork industry for many years joined the campaign to advocate for pigs, it was enough to tip the scales. The government announced a ban on gestation crates, even pushing up the start date from 2018 to 2016.

4. What's Their Stage of Change?

People progress through a series of stages from awareness to interest to decision to action to maintenance in adopting a new behavior:

| Awareness | Interest | Decision | Action | Maintenance |

Think of an animal-friendly change you've made. Occasionally people have an epiphany that leads to new action that's permanent, but that's the exception, not the rule. What process did you go through to get from awareness to action?

Identify a worthwhile personal change you have <u>not</u> implemented. That could be regarding an animal-friendly behavior or something else. How far did you get in the process? What caused you not to continue to action and maintenance? What would it take for you to move forward?

Even if you have trouble recognizing this process in yourself, you've probably seen it in others. A student is interested in alternatives to dissection, but hasn't decided whether to decline to participate in the scheduled lab. A woman has decided to get rid of a fur coat, but hasn't taken action to donate it for wildlife rehabilitation.

Other times it may appear that a campaign or outreach effort has fallen short, as when a person urged to go veg only excludes veal or foie gras. However, the process of creating action in one area can build awareness and interest in another as people begin to see themselves as someone who cares. As Bruce Friedrich points out regarding PETA's campaign against KFC to convince the corporation to institute an animal welfare program:

> **KFC is synonymous with chickens. PETA hears constantly that the campaign has turned people vegan. The campaign allows people to align with compassion for chickens in an easy way. Now they're involved in a boycott on behalf of chickens. Then, as they learn a little bit more, they see that all chickens are abused. The next step can be for them to ask, "Why are we eating chickens at all?"**

Our job as advocates is to help people through every stage until they take and maintain action. Targeting them by the stage they're in is the most powerful form of segmentation. We'll examine the process in reverse order, because most advocates underestimate the importance of supporting maintenance and focusing on people closer to action.

Supporting the Maintenance Stage

Successful businesses know that it may cost eight times as much to attract a new customer as it does to retain a current customer. That's why credit card companies waive fees for good customers, and you see so many loyalty or points programs from businesses that want to keep people coming back for more.

Few animal-friendly actions are one-time only. A family who skips the animal-based circus one year decides to go the next. Although you can only spay or neuter an animal once, people acquire more and may not get them altered. Keeping people on track should be a priority.

Sometimes it's as easy as saying "thank you." Does your local restaurant offer great veg options? Did your representative vote for an anti-cruelty measure? Did a reporter run a great story on an animal issue? (Karen Dawn's DawnWatch[82] shares positive coverage in the U.S. and how to communicate appreciation). Recognizing what people are doing right is an easy and effective way to encourage them to keep it up and to do more.

Other efforts are more involved. In 2008, the Chicago City Council overturned the foie gras ban it passed in 2006. Kath Rogers of the Animal Protection and Rescue League is working to make sure that California's ban as of 2012 won't suffer the same fate. She's contacted almost all the restaurants in the state that serve foie gras, letting them know about the ban, and asking them to stop serving it now.

She begins by making them aware that ducks and geese used in foie gras production are force fed for weeks until their livers become unnaturally enlarged. She also shares information on worker abuse and environmental damage. Kath removes barriers by explaining that these are not small, family-run, artisanal farms. From an initial mailing, to follow-up calls and visits, she and her team of activists establish an ongoing relationship, always being respectful and personable. They're also persistent and let the chefs or managers know that people are protesting restaurants that serve foie gras.

The campaign has moved many chefs from knowing nothing about foie gras cruelty to taking the dish off the menu. As foie gras-free becomes the norm, Kath and her team reduce the risk of the measure being overturned.

Veg advocates can benefit from shifting more focus to the maintenance phase. Some animal advocates criticize local vegetarian societies for not doing enough activism. They feel that providing presentations and social activities for existing vegetarians or vegans doesn't really help animals. However, keeping current veg*ans, especially new ones, enjoying their lifestyle is very valuable.

MMR Research Worldwide found in 2010 that about 10% of the UK population was lapsed vegetarians, with the leading reasons for going back to meat being concerns about health and nutrition.[83] A CBS News poll in 2005 estimated three times as many lapsed vegetarians in the U.S. as current plant-based eaters. Research by Hal Herzog and Morgan Childers revealed that health concerns ranked as the top cause for people to revert, followed by "hassles" such as finding good produce, cost, preparation time, and social situations.[84]

Jack Norris, Registered Dietitian and Cofounder of Vegan Outreach, reinforces the need to understand why people might give up on eating vegetarian or vegan.

> **Who can blame someone for eating meat if they felt terrible as a vegan ...we believe animals have a right not to be killed, but there would be a very strong incentive to reshape such views if we felt miserable if we didn't eat animal flesh.[85]**

Jack emphasizes the importance of providing sound nutritional information, such as about protein, calcium, and B12. He and Virginia Messina, MPH, RD, co-authored Vegan for Life to help new and experienced vegans ensure they're getting the best nutrition.

I've often wondered whether partnering with a company such as eDiets.com that for a fee provides weekly menus and shopping lists that users can set to include vegetarian or vegan options would help more people successfully maintain a healthy veg lifestyle. That's just one more idea in an area where we need additional research, planning, and testing to determine what could work.

Targeting People Who Are Closer to Action

After the maintenance group, those closest to taking action are the next most important target. We need to "close the deal" with people who are interested or deciding. Getting them to change builds the critical mass we need to reach Gladwell's tipping point.

In the introduction, I touched on the advantages of tabling at health fairs rather than in the tourist area. At health fairs, many people were very interested in and even deciding about eating more veg food. Spending time to help them would provide a higher return for animals than talking to people who were less interested. I learned to target my volunteer time to events that reached an audience with more people contemplating action. Health fairs and environmental festivals fit the bill. Holiday parades were out.

Barriers become more important than benefits as people seriously consider change. Revisit the table in the last chapter about how to help people overcome perceived obstacles.

• • • • • • •

Mentors Move Potential Vegans from Interest to Action

Animal Rights Coalition (ARC), an abolitionist group in Minnesota, launched Vegan University to reach people interested in plant-based foods. The program helps them overcome barriers with shopping classes that show them what to buy and cooking instruction to help them prepare delicious meals.

ARC Coordinator Dallas Rising added a mentoring component when she became the organizer for a vegan Meet-up and learned that most participants weren't vegan, but were interested or deciding:

> I was excited about the discovery of a pool of people who were already convinced that veganism was a good idea, but who wanted some help in figuring out how veganism would work in their lives.... I also knew that there were some really amazing local vegans who were great resources and had experiences like having children, being from a small farming town, cooking and baking, knowing more about health issues, and so on. I asked them if they would be interested in being a vegan mentor and all of them were really enthusiastic.

> So, we put together a binder of bios and photos and started bringing it to tabling events. Invariably, we get at least one person per outreach event who is earnestly considering veganism already and has questions. We encourage them to pick someone from the book to be their contact person. The relationship can be as close or casual as the people want. The mentors invite the mentees to different vegan-friendly events happening in the area, such as dine outs, vegan drinks, bake sales, and so on.

> Mentees can text their mentor when they're out to eat with friends or grocery shopping and not sure about a food item. One pair goes hiking every few weeks for their check-in and the mentor gives her mentee assignments like 'make this recipe' or 'go buy some Daiya

> [cheese].' We had one mentee win our Vegan Iron Chef competition this year. The mentor was so proud of her!
>
> The pairs work out what works best for them, and the relationship goes as long as it needs to. We give the mentee a chance to evaluate the mentor, about a month or six weeks into the relationship. It's confidential, so if we need to address something, we can.
>
> We also have our Vegan University Facebook page available to anyone. We have vegan panelists answer questions from anyone who wants to ask them as long as they're related to veganism or animal rights in some way.

The mentors' diverse backgrounds enable them to guide mentees at the interest and decision stages through barriers such as dealing with kids, handling pressure in a small farming town, knowing how to cook or bake, or considering health issues. The program also helps people maintain the new behavior.

• • • • • • •

Creating Awareness and Interest

Because we know how to help animals, we mistakenly assume that everyone else does too. Often they don't. Sometimes all it takes is creating awareness.

For example, when visiting Malaysia, Stephanie Downs encountered monkeys living on chains. She politely approached the woman in charge, who ultimately agreed to provide a climbing platform, walk the monkeys, and let them swim in the ocean. *She'd never thought about it before. No one had ever asked.*

If you are targeting people who are unaware or neutral, focus on benefits to entice them. Addressing barriers isn't usually helpful until people have some reason to be motivated to change.

Julie Morris of the ASPCA emphasizes the importance of shelters' getting out in the community. Many residents and leaders may be unaware of local humane organizations, what they do, and how they benefit people and animals.

> People need to know who you are, where you are, and what you're about. That may include having a visible presence with adoption mobiles, participating in local parades, or helping out in the schools. It's also crucial for shelters to get involved politically. Know

your city council or administrators and make sure they know about the services you're providing the community.

Note that although I rejected parades as an efficient way to reach potential veg*ans, Julie points out that they're great for shelters and rescue groups to create awareness and interest among the public and local officials. Once again, one size does not fit all!

Because one event, conversation, ad, or flier rarely brings immediate results, it's important to make a positive impression and foster ongoing interaction. For example, an organization advancing humane wildlife solutions could invite people to sign up to receive free seasonal tips on preventing unwanted furry visitors in the home, along with special offers. That way the group stays in front of the audience as they move to decision and action on dealing with wildlife issues.

Unfortunately, animal advocates sometimes attract attention in off-putting ways. While that can bring needed visibility, it usually backfires. Rather then drawing people to what we want them to do, angry, unruly spectacles drive people away. The initial Hegins protest that Heidi Prescott discussed in the foreword was an example of creating awareness without generating interest or action for animals.

How to Choose?

There is no one right way to segment or target your efforts. Since the stage of change process is so powerful, always consider whether and how to market to people based on where they are. Brainstorm about who they are, how they think, and where the problem is most or least severe to surface other ideas.

Often your decision will be a combination across the questions. For example, the humane wildlife solutions advocates might gear toward female homeowners age 30+. They could promote preventive measures through environmental groups. To get people at the point of decision, they might also advertise in telephone directories and manage a website designed to come up on the first page of a Google search for "pest control Anytown." (Remember, even if we wouldn't call squirrels or raccoons "pests," if that's how people search when they're dealing with unwanted animals, we'd want to find a way to get our site highly ranked on those terms.)

This step can be challenging. In the next chapter, you'll learn more about how to understand people, which can also help you define how to target your effort.

• • • • • • •

Recap

Action and Audience
• Our goal is changing behavior.
• Think of people as customers for change and address their "What's in it for me?"

Create Benefits and Cut Barriers
• People change when they perceive the benefits of doing so to exceed the barriers.

How to Say Something to Someone Instead of Nothing to Everyone
• One size does not fit all.
• Choose the best people to target and tailor your efforts to them.

Achieve Impact

1. Choose one example where a business or nonprofit appears to be targeting a specific group rather than the whole population with its approach.
    • Who is the intended audience? Why do you believe that to be the case?
    • What defines the group? Who they are, how they think, where the problem is most or least severe, what stage of the decision-making process they're in or some combination?
    • What does the business or nonprofit do to appeal to that group that might not appeal to another group?

2. Use the four questions to brainstorm at least three different ways you could define a group to target.
    • Who are they?
    • How do they think?
    • Where is the problem most or least severe?
    • What's their stage of decision-making?

3. Choose one of the groups you identified and note some ideas on how you could tailor your approach to be more effective in moving them to action.

Chapter 7

I Am Not My Target Audience

In this chapter:
- As an animal advocate, you're different from the people you're trying to reach, so it's difficult for you to know what will persuade them.
- Market research enables you to learn about what motivates people.
  - Research can be as simple as asking good questions and listening to the answers.
  - You may find valuable, free data within your own organization, at HumaneSpot.org, from government, and even from opposition.
  - If none of these sources meets your needs, consider customized efforts such as interviews, focus groups, or surveys to gain insight that will make the difference for your campaign or program.
- Testing and piloting let you see what is and isn't working before you launch something on a large scale.
- Research, testing, and piloting can not only be affordable but also save you money, time, and energy, making these efforts some of the best investments you make for animals.

• • • • • • •

Do you think you can tell which ad would be most effective to change people's behavior?

Take a look at the animal in the ad on the next page on the left that The Fund for Animals developed to persuade women not to wear fur. If people saw this adorable little fluff ball and realized that coats come from such lovable creatures, they wouldn't consider buying fur, right?

Copyright The Fund for Animals

Wrong. The Fund engaged the Humane Research Council to ask fur wearers what they thought. The ad engendered little sympathy for animals or motivation to avoid fur. The participants reacted negatively to the chinchilla, likening him to a rat and calling him "vermin."[86]

How about the bunny on the right? Surely, a cute animal associated with children's books and Easter would make a compelling representative!

Ah, no. While the women reacted more favorably to the rabbit, they weren't universally positive. HRC reported these two comments from participants:

> [T]he way I was raised, my father used to go hunting for rabbits, so we used to eat the rabbits ... so it doesn't bother me.

> I ate the rabbit and I liked it too.

Maybe this bobcat? Hmmm, that's a wild animal, less familiar, perhaps more threatening...

Copyright The Fund for Animals

The bobcat was the winner! People made the association between the young animal and kittens.

It's a baby, it's precious looking, and it looks like a house cat.

[It has a] sad look, like you know, 'what are you doing to me?' kind of thing.

Was the bobcat ad your favorite? Would you have predicted that it would be the most successful of the three to discourage people from wearing fur?

Don't feel badly if you wouldn't have made the right selection! You have a handicap here that's almost impossible to overcome...

You Are Not Your Target Audience

By virtue of being an advocate for animals, you are different from the people you are trying to influence. After all, if they thought like you do, they'd have already adopted animal-friendly behaviors and you wouldn't be reading about how to get better results!

They don't behave like you, because they don't think like you. So using what you like to determine what will move them will often fail.

> The biggest mistake I hear when I talk to [animal protection] people is thinking they are their audience…. It's hard to get outside that way of thinking, but it's essential. You are not the people you are talking to. They don't work in an animal shelter every day.

> - Brad Shear, Mohawk Hudson Humane Society

Feedback Is Critical

Think of how much money The Fund would have wasted by running the chinchilla and rabbit ads.

Fortunately, The Fund used **market research** to find the best approach. Market research is information and data about people and the behavior you're promoting. Savvy companies do research to help them sell their products or services. Politicians conduct research to win elections. Government agencies and nonprofits use it to find out what constituents think and how to affect change.

Note that market research is not related to research and testing on animals. I'll use the term "research" rather than "market research" for brevity going forward.

As advocates, we pay much more attention to animal protection issues than do the people we are trying to influence. For example, a 2009 study from the Humane Research Council revealed that in the prior three months, only 13% of U.S. adults discussed, heard about, or read about animal issues daily or almost daily.[87] While another 39% responded that they did so weekly or monthly,[88] that leaves nearly half the population rarely or never tuned in to animal concerns.

Because we come from a different place on animal issues, it's critical that we find out what motivates other people. Although our experience can inform the questions we ask, we need to hear from those we are targeting.

The Fund made an investment in research that paid off many times over by increasing the impact of the ads that eventually ran. It doesn't take a big budget, though, to get powerful information to increase your effectiveness.

Listening Is Free Research

They say talk is cheap, but it's costly when it distances us from people. When we talk to people about animal issues, it's tempting to launch into a lengthy speech. Is your outreach ever a monologue? You're not alone!

How well did the one-way communication work in our examples to persuade you to avoid mall shopping or eat only raw vegan food? Not so well. But suppose for the shopping example, I could ask you these questions:

- Where do you shop now and why?
- What would you think of buying some or all of your clothing secondhand?
- Some people have started to buy less to simplify their lives and to help the environment. How does something like that sound to you?

By finding out what was on your mind, I could focus on what matters to you. Your answers might suggest which message would be most effective: environmental, human rights, saving money, distinctive clothing, or something else. Maybe I'd learn that you were already interested, but needed help locating good secondhand clothing outlets in your area or finding transportation to get to these stores.

Do you see how this approach would enable me to be more compelling?

So as difficult as it may seem, whether in-person, through social media, or via email, we want to talk less and listen more. By asking questions and carefully thinking about what people say, we can vastly improve our impact.

The key is to ask questions that draw out what's on people's minds. Use open-ended questions, ones that can't be answered simply yes or no, to start a dialog. For example:

- What do you know about adopting an animal from local shelters or rescue groups?
- What are you thinking about spaying and neutering your pet?
- What would interest you in going vegetarian?
- How would you feel about using more humane options for dealing with squirrels in your attic?

Questions like these can yield responses that enable you to fine-tune your approach and deliver a more on-target message.

You'll probably find that asking questions rather than talking at people makes them more receptive to what you have to say. You'll build a stronger relationship. That puts you in a position to help people move from awareness to interest to decision to action and maintenance. Of course, that only happens if you truly listen to and acknowledge what people say. It's not about arguing or proving them wrong. Also, be careful that you don't make them feel you're interrogating them!

The most critical element in effective communication is LISTENING.

– Jaine Ackley, past instructor for Humane Society University

• • • • • • •

Bob Leonard Gets a Surprising Answer

After a mid-life reassessment and the death of his beloved dog, Bob Leonard began a transition away from his 20-year business career to pursue a life in animal advocacy.

At the first meeting of Delaware Action for Animals (DAA) that he attended, Bob learned that the state was proposing to expand the beaver-hunting season to address complaints about the animals. He agreed to lead the fight against the change. Bob describes the process he and his colleagues used, and have continued to use, in an article at the Beavers: Wetlands and Wildlife website.[89]

Research by listening. DAA explores potential campaigns by trying to determine what's going on and using that knowledge to focus on winnable situations.

> To find out what is driving new initiatives, we've learned to just flat out ask for the real story and we typically get it. In the case of the new beaver season, less than 100 trappers had convinced the state to include this in a major wildlife regulation overhaul....
>
> Because we clearly understood [the situation], we entered into [it] with confidence that we could be successful, and we ultimately were. Conversely, when we have opposed initiatives about prized game species, introduced by the state hunting lobby and supported by powerful politicians and the NRA, we have fought uphill battles that we have almost always lost. Unless simply shining a light

on government sanctioned cruelty to animals is your mission, in situations like these, it may be best to save your energy....[90]

Research using existing materials. Reviewing available information is another key step:

Do your homework... Prior to our first meeting about the beaver season, we reviewed all data in support of their proposal, plus a 125-page federally funded beaver study from a few years earlier. We entered the meeting with a basic understanding of their case and left with a clear idea of how to attack their proposal.

Research by creating new information. Sometimes all you have to do is ask ... and do a little work.

[We] asked for total access to the state's beaver complaint files. Much to our amazement, they agreed. After two days of compiling five years of data, and several weeks of talking with complainants, it became clear to us - and then to the agency - that we could prove the beaver problem had been grossly overstated.

By combining good research, developing thoughtful alliances, and showing the effectiveness of humane alternatives, DAA was able to stop the state agency from approving the expanded beaver hunting.

• • • • • • •

As Bob's story shows, you can learn not only by asking people questions but also by reviewing documentation. Belen Brisco suggests that advocates who want to advance anti-tethering ordinances begin by finding out what the laws are in their community and investigating what's in place in neighboring jurisdictions. Before activist and HRC Research Director Carol Glasser approaches restaurants or grocery stores about eliminating lobster tanks, she reads up on existing regulations that may support her case.

Research by Listening to Many at Once

What if you're developing a campaign, program, or outreach effort that goes to many people at once? You certainly can't talk to all of them individually. Maybe someone else already has. Not the exact people you're trying to reach but others like them.

Many animal protection organizations make research a central part of effective campaigning. They've conducted research to find out about people's attitudes, including what would motivate change.

You might even get good information from the people working against you. Businesses that use animals monitor public opinion, because they know it helps them get the results they want. Industry associations or individual companies sometimes post findings on their websites.

Academics and governments also have useful research. Governments have data such as population counts and demographics, and documentation relevant to specific issues. Note how DAA was able to get the complaints about beavers.

Much of this information is free. The good news is that you don't have to spend endless hours looking for everything. HRC compiles research reports and overviews relevant to animal protection in a searchable database at HumaneSpot.org. The database includes HRC's own research as well as studies and articles from around the world.

Two HRC studies make a good starting point for any U.S. advocate. The data on how often U.S. adults discuss, hear about, or read about animal protection came from *Animal Tracker*. This periodic survey measures attitudes and behaviors on a variety of animal issues. There's even a graphing tool for people who prefer charts to tables of numbers.

The second analysis, *Humane Trends*, parallels the RSPCA's work to track animal welfare indicators in the UK. The report covers 25 different measures, enabling advocates to assess where we are across issues. It compares the current level of animal-friendly behavior against an assumed ideal to see how far we've come and how far we have to go. For example, ideally all 50 states would have laws that limit owning or keeping exotic animals. Currently 29 have total or partial bans. The Zanesville, Ohio release and shooting brought the lack of uniform laws to national attention.

The scope and breadth of worldwide studies in the HumaneSpot.org database is too vast to describe fully. Here are just a few examples:

- *Silence and Denial in Everyday Life -- The Case of Animal Suffering* (International)

- *Comcast Publishes Results of Pet Adoption Trends Survey* (U.S.)

- *Consumer Decision-Making for Animal-Friendly Products: Synthesis and Implications* (International)

You'll also be able to access primers summarizing research by specific animal issue in the U.S. and links to more sources.

In addition to researching your audience, look for other resources on your issue and existing campaigns. Many organizations share data, ideas, and even materials that they have tested. Rather than take your time and money to reinvent the wheel, use what's out there as a starting point and then customize the effort for your target audience where necessary.

Your Own Data

If you're a staffer or volunteer, look into what research or data your group may already have. Kathy Savesky defined her strategy to reduce euthanasia at Peninsula Humane Society largely based on analysis of information about the organization's shelter and spay/neuter clinic. In fact, compiling and reviewing your own data shouldn't be a special project, but an integral part of ongoing management. We'll cover that in the chapter on evaluation.

Customized Research

In many cases, you'll benefit from conducting new research. Examples include:
- You need data your organization doesn't normally collect.
- You've reviewed what's out there and there isn't anything about your issue.
- You've gotten ideas from existing studies, but want to validate them with your target audience. For example, you've looked at research from another country that seems applicable and want to confirm the findings in your own country.
- You're measuring impact of your programs or campaigns

With low cost and free online tools such as at SurveyMonkey.com, it's tempting to jump right in and put together a survey. But careful planning increases the likelihood you'll get the information you need to make decisions that do more for animals. Consider these research design questions.

1. Why Are You Doing the Research?

Make sure you are clear on the purpose. It's easy to collect data that doesn't give you any direction. Focus on the outcome you hope to achieve. For example, you may want to learn about attitudes towards fur, but what you really want is to understand how to get people not to buy fur. Only ask about what's actionable.

2. What Decisions Will You Be Making?

Research should help you make better decisions. What information do you need? For example, if you are trying to increase the number of animals in your community with licenses, you might want to find out what percentage of animals are currently licensed, who does and does not license, why people don't license, and what it would take to get them to do so. Then you would have insight on whom to target, what to say, and what approaches to use. Always double-check that you are collecting data that support decisions you'll make to motivate action.

3. Who Is the Target Audience?

If you've already defined the group you want to reach, make sure that's who participates in your research. If you were planning outreach to low-income individuals about subsidized spay/neuter services, for example, you wouldn't want to conduct your research outside a luxury car dealership. That's an extreme example, but it illustrates that you can get misleading results by hearing from the wrong people.

4. What Type of Results Do You Want?

The type of research you need differs whether you want qualitative data that provides rich, nuanced information, or quantitative data that delivers statistics. Often a project will involve multiple phases to learn and then gather more data.

Qualitative for Impressions and Color

Open-ended questions, such as "what are your thoughts on hunting," are as important when learning about groups as they are in individual outreach. Interviews involve asking questions verbally to a small number of people one at a time. A focus group is an informal discussion with eight to twelve participants, usually led by a skilled moderator who guides, but does not influence, the interaction. You could also collect this type of information using written or online questionnaires.

Consider unconventional methods. When Julie Morris was the executive director of the Humane Society of Huron Valley in Ann Arbor, Michigan, she invited friends who were outside of animal protection, some of whom didn't have animals, to visit the shelter. Then she asked them to tell her how they experienced the sights, sounds, and smells at the facility. Their reactions were often very different from how she and other staff perceived the physical environment.

Social media also provide a way to gather impressions. Go where your target audience is online. What are they saying about your issue or related topics? For example, if you want to learn more about teachers, so your humane education program meets their needs, how about including a visit to educator discussion forums on curriculum as part of your effort? You might also use Google Alerts to get updates when the words "teacher," "lessons" and "animals" all come up together as web content. You may find more on other humane education programs than you do on your audience, but even that can give you useful ideas.

Because people aren't checking boxes or providing numerical ratings, it's more challenging to analyze qualitative results. However, the less structured, more complex information can yield important insight on how to be more effective.

Quantitative for Numbers

When you're looking for statistical precision, such as "X% believe…," you want to collect objective data from a large number of people. Examples might include public opinion about experimenting on animals, asking visitors about their adoption experience, or testing which in a series of messages would be most effective. Surveys gather input from many individuals, using questionnaires conducted online, by mail, in person, or via the telephone. Numerical results can help you not just understand how people think but also demonstrate levels of public support for animal-friendly changes.

There are specific requirements to make sure you're talking to enough people to get valid results and to compare differences across subgroups. That's especially important if you want to use the results to help you define your target audience. It's easiest to talk to an expert for guidance, or you might check out *Marketing Research that Won't Break the Bank* by Alan Andreasen. Although written pre-Internet, it has a wealth of helpful information to help you design useful research.

• • • • • • •

Research Gets the Vote for Animals

Farm Sanctuary, The Fund for Animals, and The HSUS used research to pass the first measure in the U.S. to ban the caging of pigs in gestation crates. Finding out how Florida residents thought about messages and messengers was a key part of capturing the 55% who voted to end this cruel practice.[91]

> We found that a simple cruelty message was the strongest. People were receptive to our saying, 'This is cruel. It's unacceptable and shouldn't be allowed.' Health and environmental messages could play a supporting role, but the lead message was anti-cruelty.
>
> We also identified who were the most compelling spokespeople. Veterinarians were very credible, as was the HSUS name. We thought mainstream environmental groups might be stronger, but people have a pretty good feeling about animal protection groups.
>
> - Gene Baur, Farm Sanctuary

Research remained an integral component in the campaign that passed California's Proposition 2, banning battery cages, veal crates, and gestation crates.

> The polling absolutely guided the messages. We tested different options that all got over a 50% favorable response, but some got 80%. Why would you spend time publicizing a 51% message when you've got an 80% message?
>
> - Jennifer Fearing, The HSUS

Polling helps determine where there's enough public support for new campaigns to succeed. It can also help secure victories for animals without the need for resource-intensive ballot initiatives. By showing elected officials that humane regulations make their voters happy and that similar measures are passing in other states, animal advocates demonstrate the benefits of changing laws.

• • • • • • •

You Can Find Affordable Help

Market research may sound like a complicated or expensive proposition. However, there are many sources of affordable assistance.

- HRC provides a wide range of inexpensive research services. Its Grassroots Research Fund provides a limited number of free projects to U.S. organizations each year.
- Market research firms in your area may offer discounted or pro bono services.
- Is there a college or university nearby? Marketing professors may take on your project themselves or with a class. If you're working with students, try to partner with graduates rather than undergraduates, if possible.
- You may have members, volunteers, or supporters who are market research professionals who would help. Just make sure you establish that they have the knowledge and experience to do a good job. Toronto Vegetarian Association has attracted experts by having both a communications committee and a program evaluation committee within its board of directors.

Testing and Piloting

Testing or piloting your efforts before launching them on a larger scale can help you identify what works and what doesn't. Recall how Emily Weiss piloted the Meet Your Match program with a handful of shelters before offering it broadly. I worked with Adele Douglass to pilot promotion approaches for the Certified Humane Raised & Handled program in the Washington, DC area. Lessons learned shaped additional efforts in New York, San Francisco, and other areas.

How about testing your website? Have you had members of your target audience take a pass through and let you know how motivated they were to act, whether the navigation was clear, and what they thought of the design? You might be surprised – even dismayed – to be reminded that we are not our target audience. What's compelling, clear, and attractive to us may not work with the people we're trying to influence.

• • • • • • •

Finding Out What Will Motivate Spay/Neuter

Stephanie Downs, who cofounded the FiXiT Foundation with Dr. Kellie Heckman, is using multiple types of research to find the best ways to increase spay/neuter and reduce euthanasia.

She used existing research to analyze the demographics of people in the U.S. who do not spay/neuter their animals. She learned that this group is disproportionately lower income and has less education. To conduct a controlled experiment, Stephanie identified that St. Croix's population has similar characteristics.

The report from The HSUS's initiative in Louisiana and Mississippi provided some ideas on potential messages. Stephanie commissioned research to explore which findings from The HSUS's effort would also apply to St. Croix and to ask other questions that would help her learn more about the best way to get people to alter their animals. She was surprised to see that the message on overpopulation that tested strongly in The HSUS's study resonated in St. Croix as well. There were important differences, however. For example, the islanders didn't use the terms "spay/neuter" or even "fix." They talked about "cutting" an animal.

Another unexpected result was that a significant subset of the population uses social media, which hadn't been a vehicle to promote spay/neuter on the island in the past. The research also uncovered that 70% of respondents would not use the available low-cost spay/neuter services at the usual $25 price. Almost the same number said they would be more likely to have their animal altered if the procedures were free. Stephanie suspects that even then additional incentives may be necessary.

> She was chatting with a local man about spay and neuter. He said it was 'unnatural' and was very stubborn about it, regardless of whether it was free or not. When she asked if $20 or a case of beer might change his mind, he smiled and said that it just might.[92]
>
> - FiXiT Foundation website

FiXiT Foundation will be testing a number of pricing scenarios. These include:
- $25 cost (Starting with the existing price allows testing the impact of new messages and promotional approaches.)
- $25 cost with $25 of incentives offered
- Free
- Free and incentive provided

The results of the testing will not only inform ongoing efforts in St. Croix but also suggest opportunities in the U.S. and other regions.

• • • • • • •

Getting the Best Results from Your Resources

As you consider how to do research and what assistance you need, think about what you can learn. How much time, money, and energy will it cost to pursue efforts that don't work if you pass on doing research?

Che Green of HRC recommends that you consider how much to invest based on how important the project is to your organization. For a small project or some simple feedback to test an idea, an informal questionnaire on SurveyMonkey.com or other research with a small group may be good enough. For a program or campaign that's going to be a large part of your organization's focus, spend the time and money on more formal research and any help you need to maximize your impact.

Good market research can be one of the best uses of your scarce resources.

> From full blown market research, demographic testing of our donors, informal website surveys to ... mail surveys ... we are constantly on the search for information to hone our message and target our audience to achieve our goals....
>
> I couldn't imagine spending one dime of donor funds without setting the stage for maximum effectiveness. We don't have time to waste or resources to squander in the race to end the killing of homeless animals. We must make decisions based on fact, not anecdote or the perspective of a single decision maker.
>
> – Sharon Harmon, Oregon Humane Society

• • • • • • •

Recap

Action and Audience
- Our goal is changing behavior.
- Think of people as customers for change and address their "What's in it for me?"

Create Benefits and Cut Barriers
- People change when they perceive the benefits of doing so to exceed the barriers.

How to Say Something to Someone Instead of Nothing to Everyone
- One size does not fit all.
- Choose the best people to target and tailor your efforts to them.

I Am Not My Target Audience
- You don't think the same way as the people you're trying to influence.
- Listen to them to understand the best motivators.

Achieve Impact

1. What don't you know about the people you're trying to influence that might help you be more effective? For example, how much do you know about:
    - Their "What's in it for me?"
    - What benefits and barriers do they see in what you're proposing?
    - How different segments of people may think differently?

2. What information might already be out there to help you?
    - If you are on staff or volunteer with an organization, check to see what you have.
    - Visit HumaneSpot.org and spend some time seeing what's available.
    - Also, think about other animal protection groups, government, businesses, and nonprofits as potential sources.

3. How could you get the insight you need from interviews, focus groups, or surveys? Use the research design questions to map out what you want to accomplish. Then explore one or more of the potential sources of assistance listed in this chapter to get started.
    - Why are you doing the research?
    - What decisions will you be making?
    - Who is the target audience?
    - What type of results do you want?

Chapter 8

Education Is Not Enough

In this chapter:

- While effective messages are important, they're only part of a successful change effort. Consider product, price, place, and partnerships as well as promotion.
    - Lowering price, whether that's money, time, or energy costs for your audience, can increase the number of people that take action. Use existing research or your own efforts to determine whether offering products and services for free affects how people value them.
- By defining action and audiences, assessing benefits and barriers, choosing targets, and using research, you lay the foundation to identify the best messages.
    - Even individual advocates can benefit from thinking through their messages.
    - The *strategic message grid* will help you refine your message by considering how to position the behavior you're advocating against alternatives.
    - Use the *creative brief* format to summarize your plans. You'll be more effective and may save time and money by avoiding rework on your print and online materials.
- Follow the criteria from Made to Stick for high impact communications: simple, unexpected, concrete, credible, emotional, stories.[93]
- It usually takes seven to ten exposures for people to get your message. So repetition, repetition, repetition is key.
    - Research can tell you if your communications work or need change.
- The steps in the ACHIEVEchange process should also guide your approach to social media, media outreach, and unconventional promotion.

• • • • • • •

Advocates often tout education as the key to affecting change for animals. Yes, sometimes people are unaware of animal suffering and letting them know does move them to act.

More often than not, however, simply telling someone about an issue isn't sufficient. By now you know you need to target an audience, then address the benefits and barriers that matter to them. That's well beyond simply providing education.

Crafting on-point messages is an important aspect of advocacy. It's only part of the mix, though. To see what else you need to succeed, compare two shelters.

Hard Luck Humane has:
- Many sick animals
- A very uninviting shelter in an out-of-the-way part of town, and it's closed on Sunday
- Staff who don't like people
- High adoption fees for their area

No amount of education, or even targeted, benefit-rich communications, will move many adoptions here.

Happy Humane has:
- Healthy animals
- A modest, but clean, well-lit shelter plus off-site adoptions in the main shopping area.
- Friendly, knowledgeable personnel who enjoy helping the public
- Adoption fees that are appropriate for the community

Do you think Happy Humane might save more animals?

Many Hard Luck Humanes lack community support. Nevertheless, they –and you – can get better results from available resources by going beyond education. Improving across the **5Ps** of product, price, place, partnerships, and promotion can make a big difference in what you accomplish for animals.

Product

Our product is the behavior we are advocating and the benefits that go with it, as we've covered so far. Product also includes any related tangible goods or services such as:

- Vaccinations
- Humane wildlife services
- Faux fur apparel
- Alternatives to dissection
- Veg foods

These offerings influence how people evaluate the benefits and barriers of the action you want them to take. Think how a class about where to find high quality, low price, secondhand clothing could affect where you shop. Consider how much the taste, nutrition, and ease of preparing raw food would influence you to eat more of it.

Adoptable animals would be considered "products." That may feel uncomfortable. Don't businesses, government, and people mistreat animals, because they see them as things rather than as living, feeling individuals?

You don't have to use that term, but apply the same questions that you would if you did. What benefits and barriers do people see to adopting specific animals or types of animals? Are there ways you could more effectively market the animals that are difficult to place? Promoting selected ferals or cats who won't use the litter box as barn cats is a great example of how a particular "product" provides a benefit that can be promoted.

Services associated with the placement are part of "product." How staff treats the potential adopter, how easy it is to choose an animal, and whether the animal has been spayed/neutered or vaccinated are all part of the total package to consider.

Humane advocates don't create and deliver every product themselves. Otherwise, we'd need to open stores with faux leather apparel, manufacture cruelty-free cosmetics, sell humane mousetraps, and more. Some nonprofits do get into provision of goods and services. More often, however, our role is to determine a product need and then persuade businesses to develop animal-friendly alternatives. Often we're the first customers and our outreach promises a growing market.

Price

Price refers to any cost to the target audience of adopting the new behavior. Time, energy, stress, or other emotional investment may be the price of choosing a more animal-friendly alternative. It takes time to find an animal-free circus. It takes energy to learn to prepare new foods. It may be stressful to try humane instead of lethal methods to deal with animal intruders.

Of course, money is usually the first price people consider, for themselves or their organizations. Everyone loves a bargain or something free. Can reducing price inspire action?

It depends whether people believe they are getting value. Sometimes people think that something inexpensive has little or no value.

That's been a concern about adopting out animals without a fee. Research by the ASPCA, however, showed that people don't value cats less when they're free. The level of attachment remains the same. Many organizations are placing more animals using fee-waived promotions. The Edmonton Humane Society uses a periodic "Whisker Wednesday," with seasonal themes, to offer special pricing on adult cats. For St. Patrick's Day, ads promoted free "lucky shamrocks,"[94] A promotion before Father's Day offered fee waivers for adult male cats.[95]

Their success inspired The Winnipeg Humane Society (WHS). The organization's first fee-waived promotion ran during kitten season. It resulted in 154 cats adopted in only ten hours. Only two cats came back. WHS's CEO Bill McDonald was impressed with the numbers. He's considering a similar promotion this fall. When temperatures drop, good Samaritans bring in a blizzard of street cats that will need homes. WHS offers other Whisker Wednesday promotions, including a back-to-school special fee of $25.

For spay/neuter, reduced price is a little more sensitive. In The HSUS's project we found that people thought inexpensive procedures could be lower quality. That reduced their interest. However, if they understood that the price was subsidized, there was no negative impact on the perceived quality.

Price opportunities aren't limited to adoption and spay/neuter. Animal advocates often provide services at free or reduced cost to businesses, governments, and other organizations. Businesses interested in the Good

Farm Animal Welfare Awards have access to consulting on how to switch their operations to using higher welfare products. This makes change less expensive than if they had to hire for-profit consultants or use internal resources to figure out how to make the transition. Companies can become part of the Leaping Bunny program, for cruelty-free cosmetics and household products, without paying a fee. They appear online and in the *Compassionate Shopping Guide*, gaining exposure to potential new customers. They can also pay to license the logo to display on their products.

For many related products, however, animal advocates don't control the price. Veg advocates can tell people about less expensive plant-based foods, but they don't decide what veggie burgers cost. Nonprofits don't design and sell faux snakeskin purses. However, increasing the number of people who buy animal alternatives usually brings prices down over time as companies achieve efficiencies at a larger scale and new businesses compete.

Place

Place is about increasing convenience. Transport brings animals from regions with excess supply closer to people in other areas that can provide homes. Offsite adoptions feature animals in busy locations. As veg options become available in more grocery stores and restaurants, plant-based eating becomes easier. The Internet brings animal-friendly household items into any computer or mobile device.

Social Marketing: Improving the Quality of Life lists the following dimensions of place you can use to improve convenience:[96]
- Increase the number and location of outlets
- Move outlets closer to the target audience
- Provide mobile units that come into the neighborhood
- Offer the ability to purchase online, by phone, or by mail
- Provide pickup and delivery services
- Extend hours and days of the week
- Improve the ambiance of locations
- Reduce wait times
- Increase parking
- Make products easy to find in a display

Anything that makes an animal-friendly activity more convenient than the competing behavior can be part of place. For example, online sites, such as

Petfinder.com, that enable people to search quickly for available animals at many shelters and rescue groups, make adoption more convenient. Masscats. org uses a Yahoo group to connect rescuers, volunteers, foster parents, animal control officers, humane organizations, and others to make it simpler to help homeless cats.

The Safety Net Program/Pets for Life NYC has worked with Animal Care and Control of New York City to place hotlines into facilities in Manhattan and Brooklyn. Every day from 8 a.m. to 8 pm., staff and volunteers speak with people who are interested in alternatives to relinquishment. An article in *The New York Companion* quoted Jenny Olsen, who cofounded The Safety Net Program with Joyce Friedman:

> It's like having a virtual volunteer at the shelters... In the past three-and-a-half years, we've found that a great majority of people who enter shelters looking to give up their pet don't want to do so, but they're not aware of the resources available to help them.[97]

The program provides a variety of services, including behavior consultations and home visits, temporary boarding or fostering, assistance with landlord issues, help for people who have found strays and more. Many services come free or on a sliding scale basis. The initiative had saved over 10,000 pets between its launch in May 2007 and the winter of 2010.[98]

• • • • • • •

The Importance of Place - Esther Mechler

Esther Mechler inherited her love of geography from her father. This appreciation for place prompted her interest in finding ways to help animals in remote locations:

> If you look at a map of the U.S. there is a great deal of land that is still rural. There is a need for accessible and affordable spay/neuter services where there is little service and prices are high. My first interest in mobile clinics was in relation to these rural areas.
>
> High volume, high quality clinics are making a huge difference in urban areas. But we must not forget the rural areas and that we cannot sustain [that model] there.
>
> The mobile clinics can play a role in urban areas as well. New York, Houston, and many other cities also have mobile clinics to service

the indigent. These people do not have cars, and bringing the clinic to them makes perfect sense...

Once all regions of the U.S. are covered, we will have taken away the excuse - or reason - that folks could not get Fido or Fifi fixed because they could not get to affordable services. At a time when people are losing their homes to foreclosure, have been out of work for years, and have to choose between shoes and a neuter, we need to do all we can to be creative and find ways to make it easy to 'do the right thing.'

• • • • • • •

Partnerships

Partnerships can bring additional support, credibility, resources, and other assets to your efforts.

The more you collaborate with people who believe in what you believe in, the stronger you're going to be. Look at ways to partner to get a bigger audience than you can get on your own. It really boils down to finding a common thread and building relationships.

- Sarah Speare, Institute for Humane Education

Partnerships come in many forms, but successful ones require both parties to see benefits that exceed barriers. For example, Scott Giacoppo found common ground with police to combat dogfighting in Boston. No one was going to report the activity, because gang members walked their animals through the streets to intimidate people. Scott wanted to go after the offenders in other ways. He was a special police officer for animal cruelty, but that didn't allow him to make arrests for unrelated offenses. Because the dogfighters also used their animals as drug carriers and to commit other crimes, he was able to partner with the neighborhood law enforcement to go after the perpetrators. They were both looking at the same bad actors, so they – and the animals – benefited from working together.

Scott and MSPCA colleagues contributed by using catchpoles to remove the dogs when the police went to homes to issue arrest warrants. According to an article in *Animal Sheltering*:

Before we came on board, the officers' only option was to shoot the dog... That broke their silent entry because everyone in the house would wake up when they heard gunshots and the dog howling. In addition, the police didn't want to do that, because they identified this dog as a victim, as being a living creature that didn't deserve to die because of this jerk.[99]

- Scott Giacoppo

With the MSPCA's help "arrests went more smoothly, animal victims were treated humanely, and the public was much happier."[100]

Even social media followers are potential partners, an audience whose needs you want to meet.

Social media is an opportunity for small and resource-constrained nonprofits to really mobilize the base and make use of the fact that all these people want to share your message and do some of the work for you... You have to find those people and you have to really learn how to encourage them and inspire them and also give them what they need that you can provide and only you can provide.[101]

- Danielle Brigida, National Wildlife Federation, from interview with Regina Mahone of *PhilanTopic*

Engaging partners is a campaign within a campaign. You can use the steps in the ACHIEVEchange process to target, research, and reach out to them.

• • • • • • •

Jennifer Fearing Finds New Partners for Farm Animals

Jennifer Fearing began her animal protection career volunteering to clean pens at her local shelter. Now she's clearing animals out of cages as The HSUS's senior state director for California.

Coalition building was a key element of The HSUS's campaign to pass Proposition 2, banning veal crates, battery cages, and sow gestation crates. Jennifer and her colleagues took a strategic approach to choose, engage, and secure important endorsements.

Research showed that humane societies and veterinarians were the most credible spokespeople. The team prioritized gaining an endorsement from the California Veterinary Medical Association. In a series of communications and meetings, they presented how the proposed changes aligned with CVMA's own standards for animal care and use policies.

They didn't appeal solely on animal issues. Associations support the financial health of their members. Jennifer, a professional economist, showed how the measure would help rather than hurt business interests. CVMA endorsed Proposition 2, and The HSUS brought on more than 800 individual California veterinarians as endorsers as well.

The team identified other potential endorsers by looking at their messages and considering who would be most likely to respond favorably. They felt that family farmers would support the measure, because small operations don't usually use intensive confinement. They're disadvantaged in pricing against factory farms that do. The public generally holds family farmers in high regard, making them valuable endorsers.

A simple web search uncovered a list of California's organic farmers, whose contact information is maintained by the California Department of Food and Agriculture. The campaign was able to mail the farmers and visit them at farmers markets. More than 100 farmers agreed to endorse.

• • • • • • •

The endorsements brought visibility and credibility to the campaign, showing that Proposition 2 was "popular" – many people supported it. Evaluating what benefits a partner brings will help you focus your time and energy on the best opportunities. For example, Kathy Savesky began working with feral cat organizations because the smaller groups had access to the cats. Peninsula Humane Society provided the spay/neuter surgeries and cages to bring in the animals. Each organization brought assets that complemented what the other had.

All but the simplest partnerships take time. They don't always go as expected. Be sensitive when first engaging a partner as to whether the relationship seems like a fit. That doesn't mean you have to agree on everything, but is there enough common ground? How's the chemistry? Walk away from anything that doesn't feel right. If you do proceed, plan carefully to develop shared expectations. Clarify each partner's role and work together to maintain a win-win.[102]

Promotion

We'd all love to know the magic bullet of promotion. What's the best way to communicate with people to get them to take action for animals?

You know there's no right answer, because one size doesn't fit all. For every campaign, program, or outreach effort, you need to answer who, what, how, where, and when.

If you've worked through the steps in the ACHIEVEchange process, you already know the *who*. You want to reach your target audience. Thinking about the benefits and barriers they see and using research to confirm your ideas gives you a great start on the *what*.

Now we'll look at how to start turning that information into communications that get results.

What

The "what" of your message begins with what you're asking people to do – the *call to action*. Your call to action is often the behavior you're advancing: spay/neuter, go veg, buy only cruelty-free cosmetics, etc. Sometimes it's part of the outcome, such as trying one veg-free day per week. Within each individual communication (newspaper ad, radio spot, flier, online contest, social media campaign), you'd likely have a first step, such as "call for your spay/neuter appointment" or "request your list of health charities that don't do animal testing."

Some advocacy campaigns and communications have too many calls to action. That just overwhelms people and causes them to do nothing. Giving people a lot of choices, which may seem helpful, can backfire. Other outreach efforts provide information on an issue and forget to give people a tangible action to take. Make sure you include a single call to action.

Once you confirm what you're asking people to do, create a **positioning statement** or **message** to convince them to do it. The positioning statement or message is how you convey or frame a choice to your target audience on favorable terms.[103] Anthony Bellotti shares a strategic message grid that he learned from Dr. Ron Faucheux, past editor and publisher of *Campaigns & Elections* magazine, to craft the most powerful message.[104] Below I've adapted his example for you to use. It's useful for individual advocates as well as for groups. You can use it to think about talking with people one-on-one or reaching many at once.

Strategic Message Grid

Simplified example for asking officials to ban bear baiting

In bear baiting, trained fighting dogs attack a tethered bear who has had teeth and claws removed. Proponents say it's an important part of training hunting dogs, but many people come just to see the spectacle.

	The point is about... **Behavior you advocate**	**Competing behavior 1** **(including doing nothing)**
The speaker is... **You**	1. Banning bear baiting is in line with the public's documented opposition to animal cruelty.	2. Bear baiting is a cruel, unnecessary, outdated practice.
Opposition or target's thoughts	3. Eliminating bear baiting is an attack on hunting that will lead to more restrictions.	4. Bear baiting is part of our heritage and we should have the right to choose to do it.

How to fill out each quadrant of the matrix:

1. What You Say in Favor of the Behavior You Advocate

List the points you can make that create benefits and cut barriers for your target audience to take action.

2. What You Say About the Alternative

You're always up against a competing behavior. Sometimes you face opposition that's messaging in favor of the competing behavior they want, such as attending a rodeo or voting for an ordinance to expand hunting. In other situations, there's no one actively working against you, but you need to address the animal-unfriendly practice, such as chaining an animal in the yard. In many instances, the competing behavior is simply doing nothing, such as not getting around to spaying or neutering. What can you say to make this option less attractive? If there are multiple competing behaviors, add columns for each.

3. What Your Opposition Will Say About the Behavior You Advocate

When you're up against opposition, such as puppy mill operators, factory farming concerns, hunters, and fur sellers, list what you believe they'll say about the behavior you're advocating. What barriers will they try to create in the minds of people you're asking to take animal-friendly action? Consider what you may need to counter.

Even if you don't have anyone working actively against you, what might your target audience be thinking against your proposed action? What barriers do they see? Your research should help you fill in this section.

4. What Opposition Will Say About the Behavior It Advocates
What will your target audience hear from the people or organizations protecting the animal-unfriendly behavior? Alternatively, what are people telling themselves about the benefits of continuing the harmful action or just doing nothing?

Note how the grid enables you not only to come up with a good message but also to identify one that can work compared to counter-arguments, whether originating from opposition or simply in people's minds. For example, the message "Cage-free eggs are the humane and reasonable choice, and eggs from hens raised in battery cages are cruel and unnecessary,"[105] not only forces the egg industry to defend or deny cruelty but also anticipates its likely message that cages are necessary.

Go back through each box multiple times as needed to refine your thinking. When you've made a complete list in each quadrant, choose the one or two most compelling points for your message. Less is more. A laundry list of every possible reason people should act for animals detracts from your effectiveness. Testing your possible messages, along with messages that opposition may use, with your target audience is crucial in helping you determine your top choice.

Creative Brief
The creative brief is a short summary of key points about your campaign, program, or outreach that you use to guide the development of all communications. Putting together these highlights shouldn't take long if you've been writing up your analysis and ideas at each step of the ACHIEVEchange process. The time to create a one-to-three page overview pays off many times over in more effective, less expensive communications.

The creative brief helps ensure that communications are on-point and consistent. Without this anchor document, it's easy for your website, one-on-one outreach, publicity, and other efforts to get off track or have conflicting messages. Individuals encounter these pitfalls as well, so the creative brief is for you too.

Groups and organizations can reap additional benefits from the creative brief:

- It's easier to work out disagreements at this stage rather than as you develop copy (text) and design for materials or online.
- If you work with outside writers or designers, clear direction up front avoids rework, saving you time, money, and energy.
- If you are seeking pro bono help, having a well thought-out, clearly articulated creative brief might attract more and better assistance.

Advertising agency veteran Sharie Lesniak introduced her version of the creative brief to the Animal Protection Institute, now part of Born Free USA:

Many people get far down the path of creating a communication without really knowing what their goal is.

Without a creative brief, you are also potentially talking to the wrong person or saying the wrong thing, so your message isn't getting out there in an effective way. You may be talking to no one.

Thinking through the creative brief helps you avoid these problems. It can also give you confidence to push the envelope more in developing the actual communications pieces.

Several questions from Sharie's creative brief appear in the list below:

Action and Audience
- What one behavior are you advocating? Remember not to confuse people with multiple action requests.
- Is there an interim step for people to take, such as contacting us or trying out a behavior in a more limited way to start?

Create Benefits and Cut Barriers
- What are the one or two most compelling benefits to make the target take action?
- Why should the target believe the benefits? Provide the backup facts or where to find them.
- What barriers must you address to inspire change?

How to Say Something to Someone Instead of Nothing to Everyone
- Who is the target audience? Describe them by who they are, how they think, whether they represent the most or least serious part of the problem, and/or where they are in the decision-making process. For businesses and government, try profiling both the organization and the individual decision-makers, if known.

I Am Not My Target Audience
- What research highlights provide additional insight on the target audience, benefits and barriers, or messaging?
- Once you have preliminary communications, test them with members of the target audience.

Education Isn't Enough
- What is the message?
- What facts about product, price, place, or partnerships should be included?

Voice Matters (next chapter)
- What tone should the copy have?
- What look and feel should the communications have?

> We were going off intuition when developing our website. We didn't think about and clearly plan for our target audiences. That created an enormous flaw in our draft site, something that could really have undermined its purpose had we launched. Reviewing questions from the creative brief changed the entire structure and flow of the information. The difference was amazing.
>
> - Ruth Steinberger, SpayFIRST!

For a website that addresses multiple audiences, you should complete a creative brief for each audience. Use them to guide pages of the site targeted to each audience. For pages that cross over, such as the home page, look for common elements in the creative briefs or use different sections within the page to direct people to the right message. For example, you could have the following section headers:
- Look good and feel great with cruelty-free cosmetics
- Help others wear a happy, humane face

The first speaks to a public audience while the second addresses animal advocates.

How

Now that you've worked through the what, how are you going to get across your message? A complete guide to writing text and designing materials would be a book in itself. However, <u>Made to Stick: Why Some Ideas Survive and Others Die,</u> by Chip Heath and Dan Heath, defines six characteristics of ideas that take hold: simple, unexpected, concrete, credible, emotional, and stories.[106] Use these criteria to develop and refine your talking points, flyers, brochures, ads, blogs, websites, and other communications.

Simple

Rather than overwhelming people with endless reasons to act, we must choose a brief message with high impact.
For example, recall that HRC found that including animal, health, and environmental messages was less effective than focusing on a single aspect.

Unexpected

Surprise gets attention, while generating interest and curiosity retain it.
Mississippi Spay & Neuter volunteer Doug Arp spent a day in a "pen for Rabid Dogs," foaming at the mouth (fake foam) to draw public and media attention to the issue and to the organization's rabies event.

Concrete

Abstract, ethereal concepts don't connect. Tangible appeals to the human senses, such as images, are far more relatable.
Research for the The HSUS Gulf spay/neuter project found that euthanasia statistics alone weren't enough to motivate spay/neuter, because it left room to assume these were strays or other people's animals. Linking the message to the offspring of a person's own dog or cat made the issue concrete and compelling.

Credible

If people don't believe a message, they won't act on it.
When we use inaccurate information we undermine not only our own credibility but also that of everyone else working for animals.

> **If we want to be respected as experts, than we need to give out information that is accurate and doesn't just play into common mythology.**
>
> - Julie Morris, ASPCA

While people have high regard for humane organizations as spokespeople for animal welfare issues,[107] they place more trust in veterinarians on animal health and doctors for human health. Physicians Committee for Responsible Medicine brings together healthcare professionals who speak based on science and research to deliver a highly credible message on plant-based eating.

Maintaining credibility is another reason not to hit people with too many messages. If any one of your messages seems hard-to-believe, it undermines the effectiveness of all your points.

Emotional

We respond more to what we feel than what we think.
That's why appeals about an individual animal so often capture the imagination more than the thought of hundreds, millions, or even billions facing a similar plight.

Stories

Stories provide both entertainment and instruction in a way that draws in the audience. The audience may mentally become part of a good story, envisioning the scenes in their mind.
Many organizations use the stories of individual animals to inspire the public, advocates, and donors. Shelters share tales of rescued animals. Sanctuaries describe how their residents came into their care. The story of how you got involved in animal protection or adopted an animal-friendly behavior can also engage others:

> **...people love Personal Stories. By framing your advocacy message in the form of a Personal Story of how you became aware of animal suffering, and what led you to change, you engage people's interest without threatening them. You show by example that it's possible and liberating to change one's habits into something new and better.**
>
> - Karen Davis, United Poultry Concerns, *Poultry Press*, summer 2011

Made to Stick is a great read. Several animal protection advocates have also written books about effective messaging. Please see the *Resources* section for more information.

When

How long should you run with the same message?

As long as it's effective.

As advocates, we often get tired of our messages and materials before our target audience does. People usually need to hear a message seven or more times before it really registers, let alone before they're convinced to act. Unless you have a big budget for intensive outreach or are working with a very tiny audience, that doesn't happen quickly. Don't swap out or abandon a message prematurely. Remember, "I am not my target audience." The only way to know if a message or communication is working is through research.

Are you trying to influence family or friends? They're not always the best targets, even if they're the closest. If you're engaging anyone one-on-one, telling them something seven or more times in short order isn't effective advocacy... it's nagging. So look for less direct ways to repeat the message: share websites, articles, or books; invite people to events; connect via social media; or create an ongoing dialog in some other way. Give people space to think through issues and come to you with questions and feedback. Reflect on the response you're getting to determine if your efforts are productive.

Where

It's exciting to get animal friendly messages on TV and radio, as well as in the newspaper. Websites and social media are also popular places to promote. All these methods can be very effective. Less glamorous efforts such as holding events in targeted neighborhoods, putting up posters in community centers, and even going door to door may be better to reach people who don't access electronic and print media. Research can help you learn where to promote. What forms of media does your target audience use? How would they like to receive information on your issues?

The specifics of using different media vary. When you're clear on what you want to say, how, and to whom, you're ready to work with people who have that expertise.

Social Media

The ACHIEVEchange process is as important for social media as it is for print, radio, and TV. It doesn't cost money to be on social media, but it does cost time. Gaining a lot of followers isn't enough. If your efforts aren't moving anyone to action, you'd do better to spend your time elsewhere.

Social media add a new dimension: interaction. Engaging people creates an ongoing relationship you can use to foster and sustain behavior change. To do that, you need to create a dialog rather than just broadcast your information. Questions are an easy way to do that. Try a little informal open-ended research by asking about something you'd like to know. Provide a tip, share a blog post, or pass along a link and ask people what they think or what they've done.

Stephanie Redcross of Vegan Mainsream recommends guest blogging as a great free way to extend your reach and build your audience. Blogs need quality content, so you're providing a benefit if you can reliably bring fresh, relevant, accurate posts. To determine which blogs to approach, go back to your target audience and think about what they might read. For instance, if you were promoting veg to women in their 30s who have kids, how about blogs on parenting or healthy eating? To place older dogs and cats, you might find blogs geared to seniors or their adult children. Local blogs especially need content, so may welcome contributions from hometown advocates. Working geographically makes it easy to offer or recommend related events where you and your followers can meet face-to-face.

Publicity

Don't overlook publicity in traditional media. Focus on opportunities for free coverage with TV, radio, and print outlets that your target audience uses. Research what types of stories each outlet features and what topics different reporters cover. Remember to ask around to find out if any of the journalists are particularly animal-friendly.

Once you've pinpointed the best contacts, Anna West of The HSUS recommends calling to see if they'd like to get together, so you can introduce yourself, maybe over coffee. (Check if the reporter is on deadline and offer to call back later if so.) Don't take it personally if busy journalists don't want to meet, but prefer a brief chat or that you just send some information.

If you do get together keep it casual and look for ways to connect. Does the reporter have an animal? Ask how you can be helpful to them in providing information.

Laura Maloney took this proactive, cooperative approach when she started as executive director of Louisiana SPCA. She contacted every news outlet and asked to meet with the producers to introduce herself. Rather than asking for what she wanted from them, she offered what she could do for them. Did they need last minute guests because of cancellations? She would come in on short notice. She was also honest about the mistakes the organization had made in the past, while focusing on plans for the future. Over time, she had regular spots on the morning news for one TV station and the noon show for another. She wrote the pet column for the newspaper. This publicity increased LA/SPCA's visibility and enhanced the organization's image.

If the media contacts you, you have to be ready to drop everything and get them what they need right away. Sometimes even fifteen minutes is the difference between whether you make a story or they include someone else.

Innovative Promotion

Add some unconventional approaches to your promotion mix to attract attention as well. Look for ideas that are relevant and draw people to you.

> **Put creative things into your community. Maybe there's a way to work with an improv group to do some street theater. Always try to think outside the box. If you can't yourself, collaborate with creative thinkers to find different ways of getting your message across.**
>
> **- Sarah Speare, Institute for Humane Education**

• • • • • • •

Recap

Action and Audience
- Our goal is changing behavior.
- Think of people as customers for change and address their "What's in it for me?"

Create Benefits and Cut Barriers
- People change when they perceive the benefits of doing so to exceed the barriers.

How to Say Something to Someone Instead of Nothing to Everyone
- One size does not fit all.
- Choose the best people to target and tailor your efforts to them.

I Am Not My Target Audience
- You don't think the same way as the people you're trying to influence.
- Listen to them to understand the best motivators.

Education Isn't Enough
- It takes more than telling people about a problem to inspire them to act.
- Build your efforts considering product, price, place, and partnerships as well as promotion.

Achieve Impact

1. Review the barriers to change that you saw when considering avoiding major retailers and malls or eating only raw food.
   - For each concern, was it a product/service, price, place, or promotion problem?
   - How could an advocate have used the 5Ps to be more persuasive?

2. Identify two ways you could be more effective by using product/service, price, place, or partnerships.

3. Review the strategic message grid, the creative brief, and the Made to Stick criteria. While you'll want to spend time to go through these processes in detail, identify at least two ideas that come to mind now about how you could improve your communications.

Chapter 9

Voice Matters

In this chapter:
- If we are the animals' voice, we must speak in a way that helps them.
  - People don't like criticism. They will resist and retaliate, rather than change their behavior.
- How we look, how we sound, and how we come across are essential to whether people listen to us and how seriously they consider what we have to say.
  - Protests can be effective, but employ them selectively and plan thoroughly, so their benefits outweigh the risk of negative public perception.
- Word-of-mouth is one of the best forms of promotion for advocates and nonprofits because it's free and credible.
  - Standout service experiences or positive interactions can inspire people to spread the good word for animals.
  - Bad encounters move people to tell even more people what happened.
  - When you speak to someone or engage on social media, keep in mind that you may be reaching many more.
- Constantly focusing on the negative drains our energy, brings down people around us, and drives away those we want to influence. Though it may be challenging, choose a positive perspective to keep the emphasis on helping animals.
- Put on your own oxygen mask first. Taking care of yourself doesn't detract from your work for animals. It keeps you healthier, more effective, and in it for the long haul.

• • • • • • •

We say that we are the animals' voice. Do we always speak in a way that helps them?

• • • • • • •

What Would You Say?

…if you saw emaciated dogs in a yard? Report the residents for cruelty? Knock on the door and tell them how awful they are for mistreating their animals? Maybe something more drastic? Maybe you wouldn't do anything, but you'd be furious about these uncaring people.

When Spay & Neuter Kansas City (SNKC) got a call from neighbors, Founder and Executive Director Michelle Rivera took the unusual step of joining her colleague to visit. When a woman came to the door, she understood why they were there. She explained that she'd recently lost her job. The dogs were getting only a tiny portion of people food each day.

> **They get two tablespoons of macaroni and cheese a day, because that's what we get. These dogs are getting as much food as the rest of the family.**

Michelle could have pressured to have the dogs relinquished or removed. However, her approach is to try to keep animals in their homes. She shared food from SNKC's food pantry. She also used the group's Facebook page to raise $500 for groceries for the family.

No humane organization can take responsibility to permanently sustain needy animals and their caretakers. Nevertheless, efforts like Michelle's are helping people keep their animals while they ride out the economic storms that have battered so many.

• • • • • • •

Berating People Rarely Gets Results

It's easy to get upset when we witness cruelty and neglect. Didn't the woman deserve severe treatment for not doing more to help the dogs?

> **[T]he reality is that that doesn't necessarily benefit the animal…. The animal doesn't enjoy a sense of revenge or delight [when we treat someone harshly].** [108]
>
> - Sherry Schleuter, former "animal cop," quoted by Jill Howard Church in *Speaking Out for Animals*, Kim W. Stallwood, editor

It might even have hurt the dogs. If Michelle or her colleague had criticized the woman, how might she have responded? She might not have accepted the food. Maybe she would have given up in frustration and not fed them at all or turned them loose to fend for themselves.

> **You must sell to your customer's needs, and not your own. Sometimes, those needs may strike you as unacceptably narrow and parochial, but you must avoid casting judgment on them, as that will only alienate your customer. (Even if you don't voice your judgment, people can usually tell....)**[109]
>
> - Hillary Rettig, <u>The Lifelong Activist: How to Change the World Without Losing Your Way</u>

If you're still having trouble envisioning yourself acting as compassionately as Michelle did, think about how well hostility would work if you were on the receiving end. When you read the two sample advocacy pieces about shopping and raw food, did you have any negative reaction? Were you uncomfortable that you were being judged or put on the spot? How about if someone shouted angrily at you when you didn't agree to change your actions?

> **No one likes to be criticized. And rather than diminish what we criticize, our criticism often only serves to expand it. To criticize means to find fault with someone or something. And when we criticize someone, they feel a need to justify their behavior. Justification arises when a person feels that an injustice has occurred. To them, the criticism is an injustice, and they strike back with whatever means they have.**[110]
>
> - Will Bowen, <u>Complaint Free World: How to Stop Complaining and Start Enjoying the Life You Always Wanted</u>

In <u>Strategic Action for Animals</u>, Melanie Joy discusses how a student of hers engaged a classmate on veganism using a positive, nonjudgmental approach. Initially the woman focused on what they had in common: The woman was a peace activist and her classmate was involved in human rights issues. Over time, she began to introduce animal rights, handling his questions patiently and thoughtfully. She shared not only why she had become vegan but also how. Her positive approach attracted his interest rather than putting him on the defensive. Eventually the young man became a supporter of animal rights.[111]

"Voice" applies not just to verbal engagement but also to the tone of written materials. In the chapter, "Putting it All Together," we'll see how voice made the difference for an ad that could have induced guilt, but was instead highly effective to motivate spay/neuter. Keep tone in mind when writing letters.

If you're angry or something upsets you, write a letter. Don't get hysterical or emotional. Share calmly why you're disappointed or upset. A good letter can be a highly effective form of activism and make a difference.

- Lana Lehr, RabbitWise

Engaging People to Act

Often people want to do the right thing. In other situations, they don't want to even think about it. That's why we need to do what we can to motivate them to listen.

When Alan Darer interned with Mercy For Animals during college, he learned there's a lot more to leafleting for veg eating than pressing paper into people's hands. MFA's Matt Rice taught him that smiling, being friendly, making eye contact, how you stand, and what you wear affect your impact.

People are trying to find any way they can to not listen to what we have to say, because it means they would have to change their lifestyle. They're looking for a chance to say, 'I'm going to disregard what that person said, because they are dressed differently or they were rude to me.'

–Alan Darer

In their book, The Animal Activist's Handbook,[112] Matt Ball, Cofounder of Vegan Outreach, and Bruce Friedrich elaborate on the role of appearance in getting people to engage. They cite Malcolm Gladwell's Blink regarding how quickly people form impressions and make decisions about others. How we look, how we sound, and how we come across are essential to whether people listen to us and how seriously they consider what we have to say.

It's important that we choose our attire, hairstyle, and jewelry carefully, as well as our words, tone, and volume, when interacting. Maybe this doesn't seem fair. Why should you suppress your personal expression to conform to expectations? Well, if life were fair, animals wouldn't suffer the way they do. Matt and Bruce point out:

The suffering of those for whom we advocate outweighs any inconvenience we may experience in dressing in a certain way.

Positive communications, both verbal and non-verbal, give animals a more powerful voice no matter where you work on the welfare to rights spectrum. Michelle Thew and her colleagues at British Union for the Abolition of Vivisection (BUAV) combine abolitionist values with business-like interactions to fight animal testing. They're clear in their communications that their ultimate goal is to end all such experimentation. However, they also collaborate with companies that still test on animals if they're committed to creating change. BUAV's professional style has opened doors to Parliament and corporations. Now the group gets calls from people in government and business who want assistance. That wouldn't have happened before Michelle and her team instituted a more productive approach.

• • • • • • •

The Voice We Trust Most

…is our own.

Zoe Weil begins humane education presentations with an unexpected statement. "Don't believe what I say."

That's a surprise for adults and especially for young people used to hearing opinions, directions, and orders all day. She does this to teach critical thinking. Zoe believes it's important that people have a process to evaluate what they hear and who's talking. Otherwise, how can they respond when someone else (opposition advocate, business, politician, etc.) gives a conflicting message?

Zoe became convinced of the power of humane education when she taught a weeklong course on animal issues to young people in Philadelphia. She loved their enthusiasm to learn more and the profound changes they made. Some students adopted animal-friendly behaviors and became advocates literally overnight.

She's seen exciting results like this in fifteen years as president of The Institute for Humane Education (IHE), which she cofounded with Rae Sikora. Zoe and her staff train advocates and teachers to engage others on how their choices affect animals, the environment, and all people. When I took a course with Zoe, I appreciated not only the impact it had but also how her approach reflects marketing principles. While she'd never call it that, her methods treat people as an audience for change, help them see benefits and barriers differently, and include elements of product, price, and place.

Participants find this type of humane education credible and compelling. That's because Zoe, her colleagues, and veterans of IHE programs don't lecture or tell people what to do. Instead, they share information, ask questions, encourage curiosity, and foster creativity to help people come to their own conclusions. For example, the "True Price" activity might focus on a cheeseburger, a cotton sweater, or a plastic water bottle. The humane educator asks participants if the product is a want or a need. How does it affect them, other people, animals, and the environment? What alternatives might do more good and less harm?

This activity helps students and adults formulate their own set of benefits and barriers to competing behaviors. Research supports that guiding adults to construct knowledge is more powerful than talking at them.[113] As with COK's MTV ads, young adults, teens, and tweens respond well to finding out about hidden information and working through their thoughts and response.

> We need to remember that no one wants to learn or consider changing because they're being browbeaten or judged or yelled at. Most people do want to learn and grow, and almost everyone wants to be happier, healthier, more at peace, more aligned with their values, and part of a group of joyful people...
>
> Good educators enthusiastically invite people to learn new things and act on what they learn in positive ways; they don't tell others what to do or shame them... If I give them anything at all, it should be the capacity to discern fact from opinion and to be lifelong learners who seek the truth, so that they are able to live with integrity.[114]
>
> - Zoe Weil in an interview by Mark Hawthorne, author of <u>Striking at the Roots</u>

• • • • • • •

The Voice of Protest: Use with Caution

According to HRC's *Animal Tracker* 2011, U.S. adults view protest as a less acceptable form of social movement activism:

Support

Anti-cruelty investigation	73%
Using the media	71%

Speaking in schools	60%
Filing lawsuits	50%
Lobbying government officials	44%
Demonstrating and protesting	42%

Should we use protests? Yes, but we must employ them selectively and plan thoroughly, so their benefits outweigh the risk of negative public perception.

Make Sure a Protest Makes Sense

Attempt positive engagement before launching a protest.

Historically we've used negative tactics. That helped us achieve that animals are taken into account as sentient beings. Now people are willing to listen. Positive conversation and encouraging companies to feel good is what it's about.

Of course, we do have points where we need to get tough. When we find people who are against common sense, who don't want to listen and engage, we use stronger tactics.

In the 1990s, it was just about using the stick. In the 21st century, we're increasingly using the carrot. The stick is the last resort.

- Philip Lymbery, Compassion in World Farming

Research the situation to assess the likelihood of favorable outcomes.

Before deciding on a course of action involving a specific seller, retailer or facility, it's important to do your research and not rely on assumptions. A demonstration in front of a local puppy store, for example, will be far more effective if you have specific evidence linking puppy mill puppies to the store or credible and well-documented buyer complaints.

- Kathleen Summers, The HSUS, *Cracking Down on Puppy Mills: A course for advocates* (pre-release, cited with permission)

Develop a Complete Plan

Protest is a promotion tool like advertising, social media, and online efforts. It is not an end in and of itself. The ACHIEVEchange process can help you define a clear goal, the target audience, and a persuasive message.

Don't Lose Sight of the Message

Consider whether your approach will draw positive attention to what you're saying. Recall from the foreword how The Fund for Animals dramatically altered its presence at the Hegins pigeon shoot, because the plight of the birds had gotten lost in the noisy demonstration.

Alex Hershaft recommends using events that involve self-sacrifice:

> You could hold a vigil or commit civil disobedience. People see you feel so strongly about this issue that you're putting yourself through discomfort to bring it to their attention. You look like them, or their children or their spouse, and you're willing to do this. That makes them think.[115]

Match Your Demonstrators to Your Target Audience

Young women with children make up a significant segment of circus audiences. When Vancouver Humane Society protested circuses, Debra Probert and her colleagues sought youthful moms with kids to participate. Because the demonstrators were of similar age and family status, the circus-goers were more likely to relate to them and consider their message.

Be the Good Guys (and Gals)

SAFE protestors wear jackets with the organization's logo to create a unified, professional look.

> We're not angry. We're not shouting at people. The idea is that we're the good ones and if anyone's gong to be the bad one, it's going to be the opposition.
>
> - Eliot Pryor, SAFE

Staying on the good side also means being as quick to show thanks for animal-friendly acts as you are to warn that you'll protest problems. Ruth Steinberger of SpayFIRST! cites a case where an assistant district attorney mishandled a fraudulent rescue situation that had resulted in many dead animals. She and her colleagues went to the district attorney to override the lenient plea agreement the assistant had offered:

> **We approached the district attorney directly and had many influential people call him. We also planned a picket. Small demonstrations like these can be helpful, because they involve local voters and attract media coverage. As soon as he overrode the plea, however, we cancelled the picket and thanked him profusely.**

• • • • • • •

You're Speaking to More People Than You Realize

When we think of promoting animal issues, we often lament that we don't have the multi-million dollar advertising budgets of our adversaries. While that would certainly be nice, did you know that some of the most effective promotion is the least expensive? Only if you use the right voice, however.

Consider the last time you had an experience with an organization or product so positive that you told other people about it.
- What made you feel so enthusiastic?
- What did you tell other people?
- How many people did you tell, either directly or via social media?

Take a couple minutes to think through these questions. You may even want to jot down a few thoughts.

You may not have realized it, but you were doing **word-of-mouth** promotion for the organization or product. Word-of-mouth is simply spreading a message offline or online. It's influential because people believe close family and friends, as well as their favorite bloggers and social media contacts, more than they believe companies and organizations.

Every time you engage people, you can create word-of-mouth for animals. If you make a highly positive impression, people may tell others about you and your issue.

The same is true, and even more so, if you create a very negative impression. Research shows that people share their bad stories more widely than their good ones.[116] Recall an unpleasant experience you've had with an organization or product. How many people did you tell about that? Was it more or fewer than the number you reached with your good experience?

When we take out our frustrations on people, we risk generating word-of-mouth about "those horrible animal activists." So, keep in mind that every time you're talking with one person, you may be reaching many. Your winning tone, appearance, responsiveness, and attitude determine whether what they hear about helping animals supports or detracts from creating change.

Word-of-mouth is a valuable form of promotion that you should consider as part of your mix. Making sure you're coming from a positive voice is a prerequisite to making it work for you and the animals.

• • • • • • •

Spreading the Good Word for Adoption – PetSmart Charities

In 2009, PetSmart Charities (PCI) engaged Ipsos Marketing to research how to increase adoption and spay/neuter. The team designed the research to learn what people think and to help determine how PCI could best move forward to engage them. Key findings included:[117]

1. The public vastly underestimates the extent of euthanasia in the U.S. 76% of people aged 18-34 believed the number to be fewer than 1 million animals each year when the actual number is at least 4 million.

2. The top barriers to adoption were that people were looking for a specific breed or type of animal. The next reasons included:
    *   Don't know what you'll get with shelter animals
    *   I do not know very much about pet adoption
    *   The adoption process is too difficult

3. Research respondents rated "Adopting a pet saves a life and gives you a lifelong companion" and "Adopted pets can be some of the best companion animals" as the most inspiring statements.
    *   Euthanasia messages rated least effective.

4. For those who had adopted, wanting to save a life was the most compelling motivator.

- Almost everyone who adopted would recommend a pet adoption organization to a friend, a higher proportion than for people who had acquired animals elsewhere.

We felt there was a huge opportunity to educate the public about the scope of pet homelessness and do it in a more positive way. Negative approaches were not as compelling when it came to motivating people to adopt a pet. Sad appeals make people less inclined to go to the shelter to adopt. The People Saving Pets campaign focuses on the joy that a pet brings to your life once adopted.

- Sue Della Maddalena

Based on the results and these insights, PCI created the People Saving Pets™ campaign to take a positive approach to educating the public and involving them in solving the overpopulation problem.

The campaign includes upbeat activities that create word-of-mouth, such as inviting adopters to share their stories with PCI, and with friends, family, and other potential adopters. PCI features heartwarming tales on the program's website. The Facebook page encourages people to take photos of themselves next to the People Saving Pets billboards in the Phoenix airport, then post and tag them. People can also add a badge to their Facebook photos to alert friends.

The word-of-mouth efforts reinforce that adopting is *popular* and *fun*. Television ads keep the emphasis on fun, depicting adopted animals and the happiness they bring. A brief mention of euthanasia statistics at the end leads right back to the call to action to adopt. The campaign makes that next step *easy* by providing simple search tools at the website for both adoption and spay/neuter.

It's too early to measure results of the new campaign, but PCI is piloting the ads and closely tracking outcomes before determining next steps.

• • • • • • •

Did the examples of when you spread word-of-mouth have something to do with how you were treated? Customer service can generate a lot of buzz, good or bad. Companies like Disney, Amazon, and Southwest Airlines know that service is an important part of attracting and retaining customers.

Businesses aren't the only ones who can benefit from superior service, as Frank Hamilton of Animal Coalition of Tampa notes:

> Word-of-mouth is the most important part of education. People don't trust us and they don't trust animal control. We have to deliver outstanding service from our front staff. Every point of contact has to be excellent.
>
> All our people have been through training. We have Spanish speakers out front and answering phones to make sure we provide first-rate service across the board.

Bill McDonald has volunteers at The Winnipeg Humane Society contact adopters two to four weeks out to ask what people think of the service they received. He's also considering using mystery shoppers. In this program, people not known to staff and volunteers learn how to evaluate shelter service. They then conduct an unannounced visit and report on what they experienced. The point isn't to spy on personnel or catch them doing something wrong. Instead, the purpose is to identify opportunities to improve service and determine training needs. This idea could easily extend to any organization that runs outreach tables or other public interactions.

Reducing Your Suffering

If you're having trouble speaking with a positive voice for animals, it's often because of the pain you're experiencing. You may feel terribly about what animals endure and angry about how people treat them. Even though your sentiments may be justified, dwelling in negativity won't get you the best results.

To see why, try this simple activity that my long-term business partner, Sherry Essig of Flow Dynamix, shared with The HSUS's state directors at a workshop on stress management and leadership of self.

Either do this in writing or work with a partner and do the exercise verbally. This doesn't work well if you just think about it, so please take a little time to write or speak out loud.

1. Choose a day from earlier this week.

2. Describe your day entirely from a *depressed* point of view.
    • Check your watch or clock and start talking or writing for ten minutes.
    • As you're speaking or writing, notice how you feel.
    • Don't stop until it's been at least ten minutes.

3. Repeat the process from an *optimistic* perspective.
    *   Start the time and write or talk for ten minutes.
    *   Again, notice how you feel.

Twenty minutes might seem like a lot, but you'll get more out of the exercise if you devote the time. However, if you don't have twenty minutes available, spend at least ten minutes on the exercise.

If you work with a buddy, the person not speaking should simply observe and make mental notes on what's happening. Then switch roles.

Compare the two experiences. What did you notice about the two experiences? How did each perspective impact how you felt?

In this activity, you voiced what was on your mind or wrote it down, focusing on the impact. Usually such thoughts run through our heads and we pay little attention, but the result is the same. As Sherry notes:

> **We keep a running commentary on what is happening. We do it at a level of detail that we're not even conscious of. That's why perspective is so critical.**

Continually focusing on how awful everything is brings you down. It can also exhaust family, friends, and colleagues. How would you feel if you were around someone who sounded like that nonstop stream of depression? The people you seek to influence don't want to be around endless negativity either.

We often have sad information to share. I'm not suggesting you put on a happy face about the tragedy befalling animals. However, focusing solely on the bad news saps your strength and drives people away. The goal is to evoke an emotional response with our audience, not to get wrapped up in our own emotions.

• • • • • • •

No Psychic Vampires Allowed

As executive director of Bay Area Humane Society (BAHS), Stephen Heaven implemented an unwritten policy of zero tolerance of negativity. His goal is to ward off "psychic vampires," a term that a customer service consultant used to describe people who suck the life out of an organization with their discouraging comments.

None of the shelter staff puts up with carping or grumbling. BAHS hires people who are outgoing and cheerful. If new personnel complain and whine within the first 90 days, they're let go.

Stephen put in place activities to support high morale. Staff members receive $10 on their birthdays. They have t-shirts with the organization's logo. There are contests and awards for doing good things, with small prizes, such as candy, gift certificates, and cash.

These steps aren't just about making people feel good. They're about saving animals' lives. Positive people are better able to focus on mission, provide superior service, and handle change. Stephen quickly implemented many new efforts when he came on board. His team has launched new programs and strengthened the organization's position in the community. From 2009 to 2010 alone, BAHS, an open admission shelter accepting animals regardless of health or likely adoptability, improved from a live release rate of 48% to 67%.[118] (The live release rate looks at the animals that enter the shelter and measures what percent go out as adoptions, returned to owner, or transferred to groups where they are guaranteed placements.)

• • • • • • •

How about you? Could you introduce a no negativity policy personally or in your organization? Would it help when speaking to other animal protection advocates? Could we avoid negativity when talking about colleagues in the field? It's important to debate different approaches and reasonable to articulate where we disagree. How much could we gain, though, if we focused our discussion on what does and doesn't work and why, rather than making nasty comments about people? Just because that might not be easy doesn't mean we shouldn't consider it.

• • • • • • •

Positive Engagement Under Pressure

A positive voice can even help you get better results with people and groups that seem to be against you.

When Neil Trent took over as executive director of the Animal Welfare League of Arlington, the organization was in the midst of a battle with a local activist group, AWLA Hawk.

It would have been easy to go on the offensive and escalate the argument. However, Neil knew better from years of experience negotiating improvement for animals with recalcitrant officials and steely opponents around the world.

> If you sit down and figure out how to make things work, you have more possibility of a positive outcome. If you can find out what people are looking for or what it would take to satisfy them and deliver it in a respectful manner, there are very few people who won't respond to that.

Neil invited representatives of the group to meet. He asked what they thought was wrong. The activists were passionate about helping Arlington's animals and upset that the comparatively well-funded shelter wasn't getting better results for animals. They had some great ideas that the previous management team had rebuffed.

Whether the problem had been the organizational culture at the time or how AWLA Hawk approached the staff, or possibly, a bit of both, the new dialog began to turn the tide. In just one year, Neil's upbeat outreach turned around the relationship. His willingness to ignore the rancor, invite new ideas, and act on the best ones contributed to impressive gains for animals.

Local advocate Debbie Marson sent a glowing letter to the Arlington County Board that also appeared on the AWLAHawk website (excerpted here):

> Today is a momentous day — Neil Trent started at the AWLA one year ago. And the animal lovers, animal advocates, and the animals of Arlington could not be happier.
>
> In his short tenure, Neil has significantly reduced the shelter's euthanasia rate. He ended the fiscal year with an impressive 91% success rate [live release rate] for dogs and 85% for cats. But the 1st quarter of FY 2012 is even better. The success rate for this quarter is 95% for dogs and 91% for cats.... This compares to about 80% success rate for dogs in FY 2010 and 70% for cats. This is an amazing accomplishment in such a short period of time...
>
> Neil has implemented many new programs and taken many steps in order to reduce the euthanasia. In addition to his new programs like, implementing TNR, adding a vet clinic and a new vet, and waiving adoption fees for older cats, he has reached out to and embraced the local animal community. Not only has he met repeatedly with animal advocates, he has taken our suggestions and quickly implemented many of them. He has changed the shelter's

reputation to one of being friendly to the animal community and to being progressive and proactive in saving lives. I can now say that not only am I a donor but have encouraged others to support AWLA as well....[119]

Note how Neil's positive approach inspired Debbie's word-of-mouth to both the County board and to potential supporters.

• • • • • • •

You can be positive even when you're the one applying the pressure. When Ben & Jerry's failed to switch to cage-free eggs in the U.S. despite repeated meetings and calls with The HSUS, Paul Shapiro decided it was time to move the discussion from behind closed doors into the media. Public exposure would prompt a deluge of calls to the ice-cream maker's headquarters. After learning that these calls would all go to two receptionists, he sent them flowers. The message cards acknowledged that The HSUS knew these women weren't in charge of the company's animal welfare policy. The kind act helped reinforce that the goal of the campaign was to get Ben & Jerry's to act, not for The HSUS to antagonize people. The company announced its move to cage-free about three weeks later.

Put on Your Oxygen Mask

With the vastness of animal suffering, it's tempting to spend every minute trying to help. Some people thrive on all-out advocacy. However, you might accomplish more by doing less.

Trying to do it all, especially by yourself, can lead to poor eating, no exercise, loss of perspective, and extreme stress. You can become irritable, tired, sick, or burnt out. You'll not only be less effective in what you do but also be more likely to drop out entirely at some point.

As they say on airplanes, put on your own oxygen mask before assisting others. Taking care of yourself is a way to prolong your time as an advocate and get more out of the time you spend.

Elaine Adair of Mississippi Spay & Neuter (MS SPAN) almost reached the brink by starting a new organization right after losing her home in Hurricane Katrina. Leading a statewide coalition, starting a new clinic, and relocating took many hours and created many pressures.

Fortunately, Elaine took action to improve her situation. I helped her team set priorities in strategic planning sessions, so they didn't feel pulled in so many directions. She worked with Sherry Essig to find more balance in her personal and professional roles. She also established relationships in the community and brought in new board members, staff, and volunteers to spread the workload.

Although it didn't happen overnight, Elaine has strengthened MS SPAN while feeling a lot better herself. She offers this advice for over-stretched advocates:

> **It's okay to take time for yourself. Take a break. Go to the gym. You need time to put everything in perspective.**

> **Build relationships, so you don't have to do it all yourself. Now I know I don't have to be in the clinic every day. My team can do it without me.**

Taking a break can mean pursuing hobbies or joining a (non-animal) group. Interacting with people beyond our advocate friends lets others see we have common interests and are part of the community. When you help people see that animal advocates can be "normal," nice people, you enhance our effectiveness overall. That happens when you participate in a group and let animal issues arise naturally. Going in with a heavy-handed advocacy agenda will backfire.

Give yourself a break about what you can do and how dramatically you can affect change. We should have high expectations of our results and ourselves. That's how we improve and reduce animal suffering faster. Unrealistic expectations, however, only lead to frustration. Yes, we would love to have a perfect world today. Unfortunately, that isn't going to happen.

Social change comes slowly. Over 100 years passed from the time that New England unions condemned child labor in the U.S. to the time that the federal government passed regulation in the Fair Labor Standards Act.[120] Women fought for nearly a century to earn the right to vote.[121] Using the steps in the ACHIEVEchange process can bring more change sooner, but it's important to have a long-term perspective.

> **The true meaning of life is to plant trees, under whose shade you do not expect to sit.**
>
> **- Nelson Henderson**

Be the Change

> Everyone thinks of changing the world, but no one thinks of changing himself.
>
> – Leo Tolstoy

You may feel it's difficult or even impossible to give the benefit of the doubt to people who harm animals, to speak positively in all your interactions, and to take time for yourself. I know personal change is hard. I have a long way to go in all three areas.

We must ask ourselves what we're willing to do to change behavior, reduce suffering, and save lives.

> We're a movement that's grounded in empathy. That's what we're really asking of the rest of the world. We're asking them to be empathetic to the creatures who are less like us. So my thought is 'give people a break.' Maybe people would like to do the right thing and you just need to be the facilitator to help them get there.
>
> – Kathy Savesky

> Compassion is of little value if it just remains an idea. It must motivate how we respond to others and be reflected in all our thoughts and actions.
>
> – The Dalai Lama

• • • • • • •

Recap

Action and Audience
- Our goal is changing behavior.
- Think of people as customers for change and address their "What's in it for me?"

Create Benefits and Cut Barriers
People change when they perceive the benefits of doing so to exceed the barriers.

How to Say Something to Someone Instead of Nothing to Everyone
- One size does not fit all.
- Choose the best people to target and tailor your efforts to them.

I Am Not My Target Audience
- You don't think the same way as the people you're trying to influence.
- Listen to them to understand the best motivators.

Education Isn't Enough
- It takes more than telling people about a problem to inspire them to act.
- Build your efforts considering product, price, place, and partnerships as well as promotion.

Voice Matters
- How you say it is as important as what you say.
- Positive change begins with you.

Achieve Impact

1. If you haven't already, complete the activity from Sherry Essig on talking about your day from opposite perspectives.

2. Choose one situation where you held negative feelings toward someone you were trying to influence or approached them in an off-putting way.
   - How did that person respond? What result did you get?
   - What might you consider doing differently in a similar situation?

3. Identify at least two ways you could create positive word-of-mouth.
   - Think about how you could delight people when they interact with you individually or in your organization.
   - Consider tangible items to give people to encourage them, such as postcards, coupons, or gear (for people or animals)

4. What one change could you implement to begin taking better care of yourself?

Chapter 10

Evaluate, Don't Guess

In this chapter:

- "Let us ask what is best, not what is customary." By evaluating what's working – and what isn't – we can shift our approach to accomplish more for animals from the time, money, energy, and other resources we have.
- At a minimum, think about what worked best and what could have been better in your campaigns, programs, outreach, and personal initiatives. You might also want to include questions that are more specific.
- Quantifying outcomes for many animal protection issues can be challenging, but they're our ultimate measures of success.
  - HRC's *Humane Trends* report and the RSPCA's (UK) animal welfare indicators show many outcomes you might adapt.
- Calculating the money and time spent to achieve different outcomes allows us to invest our resources to produce the greatest result.
  - This information can also be useful to get support from governments, foundations, donors, businesses, and sponsors.
- If we're wasting time and money on unsuccessful efforts, that's really taking away from helping animals.
  - "Any monitoring and evaluation is better than none. Just try. Slow progress is still progress." - Mariah McConnaughey

• • • • • • •

At a rap session at the *Animal Rights National Conference*, a group of dedicated activists was energetically debating the role of various ways to create change. Many comments took the form of "I think we should do [whatever] because ..." This comes up often in many of the planning sessions I've led for animal groups.

Creativity and imagination are key to surfacing new advocacy ideas that get better results. However, most of these comments were recommending existing approaches and giving an opinion that one is better than the other.

Is What We're Doing Working?

That's where evaluation comes in. By monitoring what's working – and what isn't – we can shift our approach to do more of what gets results.

Che Green created both HRC's *Animal Tracker* and *Humane Trends* studies that measure where the U.S. stands on animal issues. Despite many exciting victories for animals, the results aren't pretty. In his 2008 article *The Death of Animal Rights*, he noted the following depressing indicators:[122]

- Shelter euthanasia has largely leveled off, rather than continuing to decline.
- There are approximately three times as many animals raised for food in the U.S. as in 1970.
- About 95% of animals used in experiments have no basic protections.

He then issued a call to question our approaches to helping animals.

> Isn't it time for animal advocates to think beyond the same old tactics and the tired messages that we've been using for the past 30 years? Isn't it time to be more thoughtful in our approach and more demanding of ourselves to achieve tangible results?
>
> Of course, there is some excellent work happening right now that's producing solid results for animals. But much of what I see in the animal protection movement involves rehashing old campaigns and relying on the same core messages.... Sadly, it isn't working, and animal advocates must break out of their existing paradigms if they intend to achieve significant results.
>
> - Che Green, HRC

• • • • • • •

Focusing on Results Inspires Innovation

Holly Sternberg, Cofounder of Compassion for Animals in Virginia, had been involved with veg advocacy for over 30 years, including volunteering for PETA, FARM, and local groups. When she reflected on how many people she'd inspired to eat differently based on what she said or what she gave them, she was disappointed. Not many had changed their behavior.

She wondered what she might do differently. She knew video brings the sights and sounds of factory farming across in a way that no talk, article, or still photo can. However, the scenes are so tragic and horrifying that people usually turn away. "I would pay people to watch it," she thought.

So she did. Holly created Pay Per View, inviting people at events or on the street to receive one dollar for watching a four-minute video. Poster board or other "walls" surround the video players (laptops or TVs) to keep them out of view for all but those who choose to participate. While airing footage in the open would seem to reach more people, many pass by or look the other way. Some get angry that they or their children have been subjected to something they don't want to see.

Holly believes that more people watch the Pay Per View set-up and consider changing their eating as a result. The payment gives people an incentive and adds intrigue. The short length seems reasonable. People feel differently about volunteering to look:

> If you have a sign that says you'll pay someone to watch something, they're curious. They also like that they have a choice. You're not blasting something at them that they don't want to see. Parents get to choose whether their kids see it or not.

The comments and behaviors Holly has witnessed suggest that people are watching closely and getting the message:

> People talk to others and say how horrible it is. You can tell they understand what the animals are going through. They see that the animals have emotions and that people do whatever they want to them and don't care.

> People hold their hands over their mouths. They tell friends and family. It's really much better than anything I've ever done before.

Alan Darer saw similar results when he and other members of Vassar Animal Rights Coalition brought Pay Per View to campus. The video stations got much more of a reaction than leafleting or feed-ins.

Many viewers have questions about what they've seen and what they can do. Advocates running the stations provide information and talk about veg eating. Alan feels that these conversations are critical to the impact on behavior change.

Other groups have adopted the approach, including other college clubs and Mercy For Animals. FARM requires people to provide an email address, so that the organization can conduct follow-up research. Although there can be a bias with people being more likely to participate if they've eaten less meat, FARM encourages a broad range of respondents by promoting raffle incentives in the email subject line. About 10% of those contacted complete the survey. Nearly 60% of them reported reducing their meat consumption after seeing the Pay Per View, according to Alex Felsinger, Grassroots Coordinator.[123] Advocates in the U.S. and Canada can become coordinators to earn income, expense reimbursement, and equipment for holding Pay Per View events. FARM provides online data by event, so that coordinators can learn from results and improve strategy specific to their audience.[124]

VegFund also supports selected advocates offering Pay Per View.[125] The group is working with HRC to explore which video footage achieves the best results. Advocacy groups have long used graphic scenes of farm animal suffering to motivate veg eating. The research project will examine whether alternative appeals, such as using humor or emphasizing hope, may be more effective with certain demographic groups. VegFund will explore which information drives the most behavior change. Learning the answers will enable the group to maximize impact from its resources and short encounters with viewers.

• • • • • • •

Let Us Ask What Is Best, Not What Is Customary

I began a plenary speech at the *Animal Rights National Conference* with this quote from Seneca, who was a Roman philosopher, statesman, dramatist and veg advocate:[126]

Let us ask what is best, not what is customary.

You've asked what is best and rejected customary practices such as buying from pet stores, allowing your animals to breed, eating meat, wearing fur, or attending circuses with animals. You prompt other people to do the same.

Like Holly, we need to ask what is best, not just what is customary in our advocacy. The intent isn't to criticize or blame. It's not that everything we've been doing is wrong. Rather, we ask what is best to learn and to work smarter to achieve even more for animals.

To discover what is best in your advocacy, ask these four questions:
•   How did it go?
•   What are the results?
•   How efficient is it?
•   Where should you go from here?

How did it go?

At a minimum, you can implement a simple evaluation of campaigns, programs, outreach, and personal initiatives. Just ask:

- What worked best?
- What could have been better?

You might also include questions that are more specific. For example, how well did you interact with the public? How did people respond to your materials?

Include people beyond the advocates involved. Just be sure they're familiar enough with the effort. You'll get more diverse, objective opinions

> **Learn from your successes and learn from your failures ... otherwise neither is of lasting value.**
>
> - Sherry Essig

• • • • • • •

From Crisis to Constructive Feedback

When hurricanes Katrina and Rita brought devastation to parts of Mississippi, Louisiana, and Texas, RedRover (then United Animal Nations) moved in to bring animals from crisis to care. Over 400 of their volunteers provided shelter to 2,100 animal victims at six locations across the three states.[127]

Although the magnitude of the disaster was unprecedented, when it was over, the RedRover team realized it offered an important learning opportunity. They wanted to know how they could prepare to do even better the next time calamity struck. I helped them implement a three-pronged evaluation.

- Interviews with 14 staff members and key volunteers covered their impressions of RedRover's presence, how staff in Sacramento interacted with the people in the field, and strengths and weaknesses in other areas.
- We created an online survey that 233 respondents used to share their thoughts about sheltering set-up, daily handling, and veterinary care, as well as the overall impact on the animals and the community. They shared their feelings about the deployment process, onsite training, equipment and supplies, communications, and more.
- This research fueled two half-day working sessions for staff and volunteer leaders. Participants reviewed the findings and collaborated to define changes to emergency interventions.

The evaluation led to a number of changes:

- The volunteer training includes more on the intense emotions people may feel, resulting in better-prepared volunteers.
- The deployment checklist and frank explanation help make sure volunteers understand what to expect and choose to go only if it's a good match for them.
- Adjustments in leadership and support processes also enhance the deployment experience for volunteers and RedRover's effectiveness for animals and people.

Evaluation is now part of every deployment. Many of the questions from the original effort are still in use today. Karen Brown sees the debrief not only as an important part of doing their best for animals but also as part of their service to volunteers.

• • • • • • •

What Are the Results?

RedRover evaluated its process to see how to deliver the best results for animals and volunteers in the future. The online survey also measured the results for volunteers. Questions captured data on who deployed, how they rated their overall experience, and how likely they would be to deploy again. FARM's work to monitor the impact of Pay Per View is another example of assessing results.

Quantifying outcomes for many animal protection issues can be challenging, but they're our ultimate measures of success.

> Our bottom line is measured by two things: the number of animals whose lives we've saved and the amount of animal suffering we've eliminated. We try to make every decision – be it financial, organizational, or campaign-oriented – with an eye toward that bottom line. What is going to do the most good? What is going to give us the greatest return for the limited amount of time, money, and energy that we and our volunteers have?

> For about two years, one of The Humane League's main campaigns was getting restaurants in our area to take foie gras... off their menu. We got dozens of restaurants to pull the dish, helping many animals.

> However, as the campaign wore on, we reached a point of diminishing returns. Most of the restaurants had dropped the dish, but those

that hadn't had dug in their heels. We decided to turn to another campaign: getting university dining halls to use cage-free eggs.

Within a few months, we realized that we were helping many more animals with the cage-free campaign than we had with the foie gras campaign. Each restaurant that dropped foie gras meant probably a hundred or so animals spared from force-feeding, which is, of course, a huge victory for animals. But getting large universities to go cage-free spared thousands of hens per day from the daily misery of battery cages. We knew we had made the right decision in switching to the new campaign, because it had a better return for our bottom line of helping as many animals as possible.

- Nick Cooney, The Humane League, author of Change of Heart

Shelters should have the most readily available outcomes data because they have animals coming in and out. Not all collect their statistics or use them to make decisions. Central Oklahoma Humane Society does and emphasizes results with personnel.

We're very clear with new hires and staff that goals are set and they're expected to achieve them.... Our perspective of success is the entire city and the live release rate, so we can only use numbers and large numbers to deem ourselves successful. Of course, we focus on stories for warm and fuzzies and making people feel good, but it's the sheer numbers we report on at volunteer get-togethers, staff lunches, and board [meetings].

- Christy Counts, Central Oklahoma Humane Society

Dina Trefethen of the ASPCA has worked closely with Christy and her team on tracking and analysis. She notes the importance of looking beyond organizational borders to save lives:

Their focus on community animals really stands out. There is no 'my organization' or 'I.' It's always 'our animals' and 'Oklahoma City's animals.'

Oklahoma City's animals have benefited from the attention to community results. Christy and her team have worked with the Oklahoma City Animal Welfare Division to increase the live release rate from 25% in 2007 to 48% in 2010.

Frank Hamilton keeps a keen eye on outcomes for Animal Coalition of

Tampa. He posts a chart that shows annual intake and euthanasia for the county, so staff can monitor the trends. They've seen exciting progress with intake at animal services falling by 40% from June 2001 to May 2011, according to data from Hillsborough County Animal Services.[128] Frank notes that it's important to focus on and celebrate small wins to avoid getting overwhelmed.

If you had told us in 2002 that we would complete 12,719 surgeries in a year and see the declines in intake at animal service, I would have said, 'It'll never happen.'

Just because you don't capture data on your issue, doesn't mean you can't track trends. Andrew Page monitors retail fur sales figures published by the Fur Information Council of America. The numbers show that fur is on a downward trend since 2005,[129] although it can be up and down some years. Imports are falling as well, according to data he tracks from the U.S. government. (Most U.S. fur is imported rather than produced domestically.) Faux fur sales are up to $250 million per year with 30% per year growth rates forecast according to Pell Research.[130]

Defining your results measures

HRC's *Humane Trends* and the RSPCA's (UK) animal welfare indicators show many outcomes you might adapt. Here are just a few examples:

Humane Trends
- Proportion of universities with human-animal studies courses or animal law programs
- Proportion of medical schools that do not require terminal animal labs
- Acreage of protected land, oceans, lakes, and reservoirs
- Per capita consumption of animal products
- Proportion of states with felony-level animal cruelty laws
Source: http://HumaneTrends.org

RSPCA
- Number of relevant government advisory public bodies (non-departmental) on which an animal welfare specialist is represented
- Proportion of schools that incorporate animal welfare into their curriculum
- Number of stray dogs collected by local authorities in the UK
- Number of investigations and convictions taken by the RSPCA under the Protection of Animals Act 1911 and the Animal Welfare Act 2006

- Proportion of FTSE 100 companies with animal welfare improvements in their corporate social responsibility policies (The FTSE 100 are the 100 most highly capitalized UK companies listed on the London Stock Exchange.)[131]

Source: http://www.rspca.org.uk/in-action/whatwedo/animalwelfareindicators

Although some of the measures don't equate easily to a number of animals, they do represent behavior change. For example, the number of relevant government advisory non-departmental public bodies on which an animal welfare specialist participates doesn't guarantee positive impact, but it's a welcome first step that animal experts have a seat at the table for key decisions.

Including measures of how programs and campaigns help people reinforces your focus on audience. For example, when planning how to end dancing bears in India, WSPA considered that each bear brought income that sustained 10-12 people. The team needed to find ways to replace that support. They estimate how many people their replacement employment program helps.[132] Numbers like these can help you with governments, foundations, and donors that want to see your *human*, not just your *humane*, impact.

Individuals can also measure outcomes. Ideas could include:
- Number of people who have spay or neutered their animals as the result of your effort
- Number who have adopted animals who wouldn't have otherwise
- Number of businesses or schools that you have convinced to offer more humane food choices and how many people eat there
- Passing a local ordinance banning circuses with animals

How Efficient Is It?

In addition to tracking outcomes, calculating the money and time spent to achieve different outcomes allows us to invest our resources wisely.

Your time is as precious as money. If you compare the time and money you're spending to the results you're getting, you can pursue efforts that get the best results.

> **At work I've got a continual question running through my head: Is this the best use of this time and this money to save lives – either right now or for the long haul? If not, move on![133]**
>
> - Bert Troughton, ASPCA

It's all about trade-offs. When we choose to do one thing, we choose not to do another thing. We can't do everything. Doing our best for animals means letting go of activities that don't accomplish as much to save lives and/or relieve suffering.

For example, The Merrimack River Feline Rescue Society ran a cat sanctuary in New Hampshire. When Stacy LeBaron and the board of directors analyzed the cost of this operation, they were shocked. Annual care expenses approached $4,500 per cat.

Because the sanctuary was such a financial drain for a small number of cats, the board of directors decided to close it. Her team found other care for all the animals and the facility passed to another organization that would use it for adoptions. The resources freed up support for higher impact programs, including adoption, trap-neuter-return, low cost spay/neuter, and vaccination services.

Information on efficiency can also be helpful in persuading money-oriented decision-makers, such as governments, to pursue a certain course of action.

When Christine Benninger started as Executive Director of the Humane Society of Silicon Valley (HSSV), she secured the animal control contract to bring in much-needed revenue to address the organization's dire financial position. The cities paid HSSV based on the intake number. Christine's analysis showed that it cost from $250 to $300 for every animal that came in compared to only $30 to spay or neuter. She was able to convince the largest city she served, San Jose, California, to invest in spay/neuter. That initiative was integral to HSSV reducing intake from 45,000 in 1993 to approximately 9,000 in 2006.[134]

Where Should You Go from Here?

The goal of evaluation is to guide future action, not only for the program, campaign, or effort you're measuring but also for any new ventures you initiate. For example, in the chapter "How to Say Something to Someone instead of Nothing to Everyone," you learned about how Andrew Page targets retailers differently based on how they think, their strategy. That lesson came from The Fund for Animals' evaluation of the campaign it had joined to persuade Neiman Marcus to close its fur salons.[135]

A group of activists decided to take on the ultra-upscale store after they convinced Macy's West to close its fur departments in 1997. The activists held protest outside Neiman Marcus stores. However, corporate leaders market the company as the ultimate luxury retailer. Executives are, therefore, willing to withstand heavy pressure over the fur policy. They might even accept losing money in the fur departments, because the salons are part of the high-end image. Until affluent customers buy less fur and tell Neiman Marcus they won't shop at a store that sells it, the fur department will likely remain. The Fund concluded that continuing to invest heavily in the protests wasn't the best use of resources.

That doesn't mean that Neiman Marcus gets a free pass. Efforts to move the company's position on fur continue, now with The Fund as part of The HSUS. According to the *Dallas Morning News*, in 2009 the company paid a $25,000 judgment after The HSUS sued claiming the retailer "violated consumer protection laws by falsely advertising two coats as having 'faux fur' trim when it was animal fur."[136]

The results of The Fund's evaluation of the Neiman Marcus campaign reinforce the importance of choosing targets carefully. It also shows the value in adapting your approach as you go.

When Should You Define Your Evaluation?

> Setting metrics is a big part of our planning, so we can show what impact we've had. How else can you know what change you're affecting? It's so important to do.

> - Sharanya Krishna Prasad, WSPA

Consider how you will evaluate a program or campaign when you design it. If you wait until it's over, you may not be able to get the information you need. For example, if you're evaluating the impact of a spay/neuter campaign in targeted neighborhoods, you'll want to capture the location of new visitors to the clinic to see how many come from these areas. You usually need to collect initial data to establish a baseline that you can compare to after the program or intervention. For example, if you wanted to assess the effectiveness of an anti-fur advertising campaign by finding out how many people were likely to buy an animal-derived coat within three months, you'd want to look at numbers before and after to see if there was a meaningful change.

Thinking about how you will measure success increases the likelihood you will achieve it. Weighing what constitutes progress helps you or your team create a consistent, clear vision. That can often surface new and better ideas of how to get there.

How Much Should You Spend?

Evaluation can start with the simple – and free – process of asking questions. Holly Sternberg focused on results to determine she needed a new approach for veg outreach. Measuring outcomes and efficiency requires a more complex effort that takes some time and possibly money. According to the W.K. Kellogg Foundation, you should plan to spend five to seven percent of your program or campaign budget to do evaluation.[137]

Many animal advocates fear that spending time and money on evaluation takes away from helping animals. Without evaluation, however, we don't know if the money we're spending is getting results. If we're wasting time and money on unsuccessful efforts, that's really taking away from helping animals.

Evaluation can also help bring in money. Foundations increasingly require proof of outcomes. Clear results motivate donors. In its annual report, Humane Farm Animal Care shares not only the number of animals that the Certified Humane program helps each year but also that the improvement in farm animals' lives comes at the cost of only 3¢ per animal.

David Alexander of Toronto Vegetarian Association notes the role evaluation plays in the success of its Vegetarian Food Festival. The group gathers data about who comes, what they do at the event, what they liked, and which information seemed most useful for them to make change in their lives. David and his colleagues use the findings to shape the offerings at future festivals. They also use the information to attract new vendors and sponsors to sustain the event.

Take the same approach you would on research to understand your audience and test approaches to motivating change. If a campaign, program, or outreach effort requires only a small amount of time or money, asking informally what worked and what could be better may be enough. For programs or campaigns that are a major part of your group's or your own efforts, invest what's needed to find out if what you're doing is working. The *Resources* section in the back of the book includes information about a guide you can use to learn more, or you may prefer to engage a professional.

• • • • • • •

You Can't Get There if You Don't Start

Any monitoring and evaluation is better than none. Just try! Slow progress is still progress.

- **Mariah McConnaughey,** *Monitoring and Evaluating Education Programs - a Key to Humane Education's Success* **(PetSmart Charities webinar)**

Don't think you have to be an expert to get into evaluation. You'll get better ideas about how to refine your measurement as you go along.

Mariah McConnaughey and colleagues at WSPA evolved their approach to assess their humane education efforts in developing countries. The program provides two trainings and other support to help teachers include humane education activities in the classroom throughout the year.

- At first, the tracking only captured the number of participants. That was a good beginning, but didn't provide any insight on the quality of the program.
- To delve deeper, the team worked with an outside expert to develop a questionnaire to measure teacher attitudes before and after trainings. This confirmed that the teachers were more positive about animal issues after the training. However, they were also largely positive before. In addition, the survey didn't reveal anything about the impact on students.
- WSPA has since developed research tools to gather data on students' attitudes before and after exposure to humane education. Although behavior change is always the ultimate goal, understanding impact on knowledge and attitudes is useful. The information can suggest where the program is and isn't working and what adjustments might get better results.

While the process has been challenging, WSPA team members in the London, Costa Rica, Colombia, Brazil, Tanzania, India, and Thailand, are eager to see the feedback.

Even before we get the results, everyone sees that this process will tie together everything we've been doing. We all want to know how effective the work has been.

We also hope to use the findings to help our relationships with ministries and governments. If we can say we've done a pilot and here's how student attitudes have changed, we demonstrate impact and garner support for expanding the effort.

- Mariah McConnaughey

Mariah recognizes that advocates often fear that an evaluation will show what they're doing isn't working. Rather than face potentially bad news, they prefer not to know. However, the key is to focus on the value of the lessons learned to help you be more effective in the future.

If you don't get the results that you're hoping for, you just have to take a step back and say, 'Hey, this isn't the best way to be approaching it.' That needs to be okay for people.

• • • • • • •

You have shown the ability to challenge conventional wisdom about how to treat animals. You've made a commitment to work for animals and to engage others. That commitment and ability to think differently will enable you to ask the hard questions about what's working and commit to pursuing what is best, not what is customary.

We work toward the day that evaluation is unnecessary, because we have achieved our goal of caring, compassionate treatment for all animals.

• • • • • • •

Recap

Action and Audience
• Our goal is changing behavior.
• Think of people as customers for change and address their "What's in it for me?"

Create Benefits and Cut Barriers
• People change when they perceive the benefits of doing so to exceed the barriers.

How to Say Something to Someone Instead of Nothing to Everyone
• One size does not fit all.
• Choose the best people to target and tailor your efforts to them.

I Am Not My Target Audience
- You don't think the same way as the people you're trying to influence.
- Listen to them to understand the best motivators.

Education Isn't Enough
- It takes more than telling people about a problem to inspire them to act.
- Build your efforts considering product, price, place, and partnerships as well as promotion.

Voice Matters
- How you say it is as important as what you say.
- Positive change begins with you.

Evaluate, Don't Guess
- We have to determine if we're getting results and learn from our experience to do better.

Achieve Impact

1. Choose one program, campaign, outreach effort, or personal advocacy activity and ask:
   - What worked best?
   - What could have been better?

   Involve other people where possible to gain additional perspective and insight. Write down what you learn that you can use to improve your impact.

2. Define one outcome measure that you can begin to track to learn more about whether what you're doing is working. Refer back to the section in this chapter entitled "what are the results" for some ideas to get you started.

Chapter 11

Putting it All Together

In this chapter:
A spay/neuter campaign and a compilation of efforts to persuade restaurants to offer more veg options demonstrate the ACHIEVEchange system in its entirety.

• • • • • • •

Now that you've learned the full ACHIEVEchange framework, take another look at how it all comes together to create success. The first example is a more detailed look at the effort The HSUS and Maddie's Fund launched to increase spay/neuter in Louisiana and Mississippi (the Gulf Coast) after Hurricane Katrina.

New Insight on Motivating Spay/Neuter

Action and Audience

Our goal is changing behavior. Think of people as customers for change and address their "What's in it for me?"
The campaign's original goals included increasing both adoption and spay/neuter. However, phase 1 researched showed that a large number of people were already taking in animals from friends, family, neighbors, and the street. Approximately 60% of households with dogs and over 70% with cats reported acquiring animals from friends or family or as strays. Another 5% of dog households and 8% for cats had animals from their own litters.[138] These findings suggested that motivating spay/neuter to stop the flow of animals would be more productive than splitting resources across two behaviors.

The primary audience was the 52% of households with at least one unaltered dog and the 23% of households with one or more intact cats.[139] An extensive research effort explored what would motivate these households to spay or neuter.

Create Benefits and Cut Barriers

People change their behavior when they perceive the benefits of doing so to exceed the barriers.

National data by Purina for the U.S. in 2000 showed that the top reason people hadn't altered animals was that they just hadn't bothered. Wanting to breed was cited next for dogs, while "too young" followed for cats. Eighteen percent of respondents with cats said they couldn't afford the procedure, as did 5% of people with dogs.[140]

Project research by Greenberg Quinlan Rosner in Louisiana and Mississippi yielded similar, though not identical results. Differences are attributable to the well-below average levels of education and income in the two states. Again, many people simply hadn't thought about it or gotten around to altering their animals. Others wanted to breed their dogs. Compared to the U.S. numbers, however, a larger proportion of people in the region thought that spay/ neuter was unnecessary because their animals didn't run loose outside the home. (FIREPAW found this reason correlated with having lower education in its research in upstate New York.)[141] Affordability concerns were higher here than nationally as well.

Top reasons people don't spay/neuter[142]	Dogs	Cats*
Not loose or uncontrolled/no need	26%	11%
I want to breed my pet	25%	8%
It costs too much	17%	27%
I have not gotten around to it	13%	17%
I have never thought about it	11%	12%

*22% don't know, refused, or other

Another question on cost reinforced the importance of that barrier:

Asked more directly, 42 percent agree (27 percent strongly agree) with the statement, 'Spaying and neutering simply costs too much for me.'

- Greenberg Quinlan Rosner, October 2007[143]

Focus group participants put the face on the issue with comments like this one:

> I have lots of medical expenses.... I have medicines I can't actually afford on a monthly basis, so this would take precedence over that. There's a real cost issue.[144]

The campaign needed to overcome perceived barriers and make the procedure possible, top-of-mind, and high priority. That required finding ways to increase the number of quality, affordable surgeries available; showing why spay/neuter is always important; and creating a sense of urgency.

How to Say Something to Someone Instead of Nothing to Everyone

One size does not fit all. Choose the best people to target and tailor your efforts to them.
The campaign intentionally did not prioritize persuading people committed to breeding or the small percent who had negative feelings about spay/neuter. Instead, efforts focused on moving to action those who were at least potentially receptive. It's possible, even likely, that some people would rethink breeding after seeing the campaign, but the team did not create special messages or initiatives to reach this segment. The strategy was to go after the "low hanging fruit."

The campaign also targeted lower-income individuals, a large portion of the population. Analysis of shelter intake by zip code and visits to neighborhoods enabled the team to match promotion more precisely to reach the right audience. Radio ads, local events, and neighborhood outreach brought the message to African-American and Latino audiences, with Spanish language materials for the latter.

I Am Not My Target Audience

You don't think the same way as the people you're trying to influence. Listen to them to understand the best motivators.
The project involved multiple rounds of research to understand the audience, test messages, and get feedback on materials. Team members:

- Reviewed existing national research on spay/neuter and adoption, plus demographic data on the two states
- Surveyed households with animals to determine source of animals, percent unaltered, reasons for not adopting or spaying/neutering, and more

- Held focus groups to learn about barriers and motivators for spay/neuter
- Used surveys to test potential messages and other proposed campaign elements
- Conducted interviews to gauge response to promotion materials
- Piloted implementation and evaluated initial results in Shreveport, Louisiana; Jackson, Mississippi; and Gulfport, Mississippi

The research provided the foundation for the entire campaign.

One especially interesting finding was the reaction to sample ads that had been used to promote spay/neuter in the past. The ads were professional and thoughtfully developed. Can you tell which one of the two below, if either, focus group participants found compelling?

Copyright The Humane Society of the United States

Here's what people had to say:

Do it for Love

That dog on there is looking like, 'Uh uh. Don't do it.'

Just because I don't have my pet spayed or neutered does that mean I don't love him?

Note how the second research participant commenting here interpreted an accusation or attempt at inflicting guilt, even though that wasn't the intention.

Pick One

I think it's an eye opener to wake you up and let you know that all of these cats are not going to make it.

I think it's more effective than the illustration because these are real.

Results for design, message, and spokespeople suggest that many communications currently used for spay/neuter can be improved:

- People trusted veterinarians most as a source of spay/neuter, with confidence lowest for shelters and mobile clinics. Spay/neuter clinics and other humane organizations can persuade more people to use their services by emphasizing professionalism and safety.
- Research participants viewed celebrity spokespeople with suspicion, other than those known as animal advocates, such as Bob Barker and Betty White. Again, veterinarians came out on top for credibility, followed by humane group leaders and animal control officers.
- Humor and innuendo fell flat when promoting spay/neuter. People outside the field see it as a medical procedure for their animals that warrants serious handling.
- Photos had more impact than illustrations, but if the dogs or cats were too attractive, people wondered why anyone would want to get that animal fixed.

As animal advocates, we sometimes talk to ourselves instead of our audience. We learned in the Gulf [project] that we had made a lot of assumptions about what would appeal. We found out a lot of our messaging was wrong.

We've completely changed how we talk about spay and neuter. We don't use the cute dog and cat or celebrities. People view it as a serious medical procedure. They want to hear from a vet and hear the message sincerely.

- Betsy McFarland, The HSUS

Based on the initial feedback, Illume Communications developed creative concepts (design and text) and tested them. A sample billboard reads:
What Happened to Your Dog's Puppies?
In Louisiana, 92,000 homeless pets are put down each year.
[Please Spay or Neuter Your Pets]

Copyright The Humane Society of the United States

At first, you might think this message is a guilt appeal. It could be if you went up to someone and asked in a hostile tone, "What happened to your dog's puppies?" or "Let me tell you what probably happened to your cat's kittens." However, using a question, a plain background, and a calming color (navy blue) elicited concern or sadness rather than guilt.

> When testing the [message and design concepts], people did not feel any accusations were being made... if people felt guilt, they reached that on their own and not through any intention of the creative [design] or messaging. People responded that the numbers were very sad and that they viewed this as a community problem and saw the call to action (please spay or neuter) as a solution and way they could help.
>
> - Annie Pruitt, Illume Communications

These comments from two people interviewed during the research illustrate that they perceived a question, not a condemnation:

> ...so you think well my dog had puppies, so I gave them away, I wonder where they went, did they... get euthanized. It makes you think.

> This is a good question. I really don't know.

Education Isn't Enough

It takes more than telling people about a problem to inspire them to act. Build your efforts considering product, price, place, and partnerships as well as promotion.

Product and Price

Given the number of people concerned about the cost of spay/neuter, it would be a waste of money to promote the procedure in the absence of affordable services. The HSUS, in partnership with other national groups, including the ASPCA, International Fund for Animal Welfare, Maddie's Fund, PetSmart Charities, and Red Rover, invested in the region as part of post-Katrina efforts. The campaign led to additional investments to make even more low-cost surgeries available.[145]

The team discovered that although affordable surgeries were in demand, messaging on price was a sensitive area. People were concerned that low-priced procedures also meant low quality. It was important to emphasize the quality of care provided and to make clear that humane organizations were subsidizing the price.

Place

Local and national groups collaborated to establish new clinics in places that didn't have affordable options. Mobile units served areas that couldn't support a stationary clinic

Partnerships

The campaign involved extensive collaboration among national players and local spay/neuter groups from the outset. Partnerships remain an integral part of the continued effort. Even organizations beyond the humane realm have been highly beneficial in reaching low-income individuals and families. Bringing events and outreach to community centers puts the message in a trusted place where people already go. If the team can make connections with human services groups in the area, that also helps introduce humane advocates and issues to neighborhood residents.

Promotion

Message

The research revealed that the most effective message was:

> A quarter of a million pets enter animal shelters in Mississippi and Louisiana every year. More than half of pets in these shelters are put to sleep or euthanized because shelters are overcrowded and pets cannot be placed in homes. The offspring of your pet could end up in these shelters. Spaying and neutering helps reduce the number of unwanted pets and pet deaths.[146]

In the focus groups, the team had learned that people assume animals in shelters were strays or other people's animals. Therefore linking dogs and cats being euthanized to someone's own animal was a crucial part of the message.

Note how the message reflects the Made to Stick criteria:

Simple. The campaign used a straightforward message about animals being put down and the possibility that "your pet's puppies or kittens" could be among them.

Unexpected. The extent of euthanasia still surprises people outside of animal protection. The link to people's own animals was new and different from their expectations that this only happened to strays or other people's animals.

Concrete. Linking to people's own dog or cat made the issue more concrete than solely referencing thousands of seemingly nameless, faceless animals.

Credible. Local humane organizations and The HSUS are credible sources for messages about animal welfare. The use of the question "What happened to your dog's puppies" or "your cat's kittens" allowed people to think through scenarios themselves and draw their own conclusions that their animal's offspring could be euthanized.

Emotional. These scenarios caused people to feel concern and compassion for their animal's past or potential offspring as well as for other dogs and cats euthanized.

Stories. As they thought about what would happen to past or potential offspring of their own animals the audience created their own stories.

The creative development also adhered to the principles, providing simple, unexpected, concrete stories designed to evoke emotion. One approach used in radio and TV depicted a euthanasia technician talking about her day as she comforted a dog she was going to have to put down. Another showed a male dog digging under a fence to reach a female, a natural act that led to the unnatural euthanasia of unwanted puppies.

Methods
TV and radio spots ran in each media market. Outreach in neighborhoods included billboards and special events. Initially the campaign used attention-getting tables or activities at local fairs and parades. Over time, the emphasis shifted to animal-focused events. The most successful venues were free rabies clinics. However, even attracting 300 to 1500 low-income people and their animals wasn't enough. When team members visited, they saw they needed to do more to move people from awareness to action.

> **We found out that some of the staff and volunteers weren't connecting with people. That was problematic. People were just getting free shots and leaving. Now we work the line to develop relationships with them, ask them about their situation, and find out if they need spaying or neutering for their animals.**
>
> **- Annie Pruitt**

Team members trained staff and volunteers of local spay/neuter groups on how to talk to people in line about spay and neuter. They found that over three quarters of people who attended had unaltered pets. They are now able to get about two thirds to agree to spay or neuter.

Even this decision doesn't guarantee action. The no-show rate on spay/neuter appointments is a concern for many clinics. The team has managed the marketing effort to achieve nearly a one hundred percent success rate. The vouchers that people get show the full retail value for the surgery based on the species, gender, and size of the animal. Advocates remind them that the voucher is like cash and they should store it somewhere safe, such as in a wallet. This increases the perceived value of the procedure. If the appointment is several weeks out, local staff or volunteers call after about a week, rather than waiting until a few days before, to see if people have additional concerns or questions. Because they've established a positive relationship from the initial contact, these follow-up conversations often surface deeper issues that could have stopped people from coming. For example, someone who at the event agrees to a co-payment may admit to not having the money. This allows the advocate to offer additional price reductions if needed.

Voice Matters

How you say it is as important as what you say.

None of the advertising, materials, or interaction ever talked about "responsibility." The research showed that people thought of themselves as responsible whether their animals were altered or not and responded negatively if anyone implied otherwise. When you think about it, it's disrespectful to judge people who may not be familiar with spaying and neutering, or may be struggling to keep their families afloat financially.

Amanda Arrington knew the importance of a sympathetic voice and an attitude of service from founding the Coalition to Unchain Dogs. She and other volunteers have persuaded people to accept free fences for more than 1,000 dogs.[147]

Amanda brought this expertise in outreach to low-income families when she joined The HSUS and became part of the spay/neuter campaign team.

> We need to meet people where they are, not expect them to come to us. A lot of animal advocates have never set foot in the neighborhoods where the people live. When you see their homes, how they're caring for multiple generations, it's naïve for us to think that the dog or the cat is the most important thing.

> When you're out in the community you need to get out of your own head. Spay/neuter can't be the only way we connect with people. If that's all you're talking about, it can turn off people. People will be wary and we have to expect that.

> The foundation is greeting people in a non-judgmental way and with respect. Introduce yourself. Ask about their lives or their kids. Then you can ask about the animal. What's the animal's name? When did you get him or her? I ask permission to pet the animal, to reinforce that the person is in control. I also compliment the animal. By doing that, I show that I'm not negative or judging.

Then I can start talking about what we do. I acknowledge that animal care is expensive and we recognize that. We know the economy is tough and they're struggling. That's why we're here. We want to make spay and neuter more obtainable for everyone. I let them know that spaying and neutering helps them, not just the animal.

Once Amanda or local staff and volunteers establish these relationships, then the euthanasia message can work.

Many people haven't ever thought how their personal decisions impact the population around them. It's really moving to people when they make the connection.

Evaluate, Don't Guess

We have to determine if we're getting results and learn from our experience to do better. The campaign has achieved encouraging results on several dimensions. By the end of 2010, there will be approximately 40,000 to 50,000 more spay/neuter surgeries performed annually.[148] In some areas, such as Hattiesburg, Mississippi, the increased procedures have led to reductions in intake.[149]

More precise evaluation has been tricky in this region and across the country. Mapping intake and euthanasia trends against spay/neuter is always challenging because there are so many other variables that influence outcomes. Different organizations may track their numbers differently. In a poor economy, more people relinquish animals because they can't afford them or because they've lost their homes. Municipalities reduce budgets for animal control. Intake may decline because fewer officers are bringing in animals. That doesn't mean a decrease in animal suffering. Amanda notes that the poorest communities may not have a shelter and residents may not contact animal control, so traditional statistics miss changes in the targeted neighborhoods entirely.

The HSUS, ASPCA, PetSmart Charities, and other groups are working together to identify how to better assess spay/neuter programs and their impact. Many clinic and mobile unit managers already focus tracking on surgeries for animals from low-income households or living in specific zip codes. The measurement team is considering whether procedures for male vs. female animals or those that live outdoors vs. indoors should be weighted differently when quantifying the amount of spay/neuter in an area. Because many parts of the country don't have shelters or people don't take animals to the shelter, the team is also reviewing whether conducting counts of stray dogs and cats in targeted neighborhoods should supplement using intake numbers to gauge the effects of spay/neuter.

Bringing the Campaign to Your Area

The firm that conducted the research for the campaign believes the results would be applicable to low-income individuals across the U.S. Local organizations can undertake additional research, if desired, to validate findings in their own regions, as Stephanie Downs did in St. Croix.

Gulf Coast Pet Research Project: Phase 1
http://www.animalsheltering.org/programs_and_services/spay_neuter/
hsus-gulf-phase-1-final-public.pdf

Messaging Spay/Neuter, Lessons from the Gulf Coast Spay/Neuter Campaign
http://www.animalsheltering.org/programs_and_services/spay_neuter/
messaging-spay-neuter-report-_-final.pdf

The HSUS offers the campaign ads, posters, door hangers, and other materials at no charge for local groups to download and customize.
http://www.animalsheltering.org/programs_and_services/spay_neuter/
spay_neuter_campaign_materials/

Amanda and her team are working with PetSmart Charities to launch a complete kit to train advocates how to talk to people about spay/neuter for their animals. The kit will include scripts, role-playing activities, and answers to common questions. Underlying every element of the kit is focusing on the "What's in it for me?" for low-income people to spay or neuter.

> We can't just try to push our ideas on people. When you treat people as clients you get back what you put out. It's a big shift for our field. It won't happen overnight.
>
> - Amanda Arrington

Make Mine Veg, Please

Many organizations and individuals have been highly effective in persuading restaurants to put more veg options on the menu. The following example highlights ideas from different sources rather than profiling a single initiative.

Action and Audience

Our goal is changing behavior. Think of people as customers for change and address their "What's in it for me?"

Charles Stahler and Debra Wasserman, Founders of Vegetarian Resource Group (VRG), recognized that making it easy for people to find veg food at the supermarket and when eating out reduces barriers to plant-based eating. VRG's activities therefore include helping grocers and restaurants to offer these options (*action*).

To do so, the team has approached industry as an audience, a natural for Charles who majored in business as an undergraduate. They know that for companies, "What's in it for me?" means profitability and growth. They show ventures from start-ups to leading corporations that there's a large market for veg foods, not just from vegetarians and vegans but also from other people looking for healthier meals. VRG also provides information about ingredients and recipes to make it easy for restaurants to serve plant-based dishes. Even the organization's name, Vegetarian Resource Group, conveys the image of a safe, professional source of assistance.[150]

VRG also assists entrepreneurs interested in launching a veg eatery, with resources including "Starting a Veg Restaurant - Food for Thought" in the business section of their website, vrg.org.

Create Benefits and Cut Barriers

People change their behavior when they perceive the benefits of doing so to exceed the barriers.

Paul Shapiro launched Compassion Over Killing's restaurant outreach campaign when he shifted the organization's strategy to include fewer confrontational activities and more strategic, cooperative efforts. One of the early wins was Java Green in Washington, DC. Originally, the restaurant had limited vegetarian options. COK's outreach helped inspire the owner to become vegan and make Java Green all vegetarian. He later opened Café Green to offer an upscale vegan dining experience.

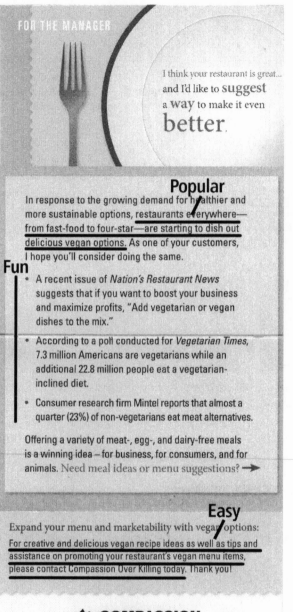

FOR THE MANAGER

I think your restaurant is great...
and I'd like to suggest
a way to make it even
better.

Popular

In response to the growing demand for healthier and more sustainable options, restaurants everywhere—from fast-food to four-star—are starting to dish out delicious vegan options. As one of your customers, I hope you'll consider doing the same.

Fun

* A recent issue of *Nation's Restaurant News* suggests that if you want to boost your business and maximize profits, "Add vegetarian or vegan dishes to the mix."

* According to a poll conducted for *Vegetarian Times*, 7.3 million Americans are vegetarians while an additional 22.8 million people eat a vegetarian-inclined diet.

* Consumer research firm Mintel reports that almost a quarter (23%) of non-vegetarians eat meat alternatives.

Offering a variety of meat-, egg-, and dairy-free meals is a winning idea – for business, for consumers, and for animals. Need meal ideas or menu suggestions? →

Easy

Expand your menu and marketability with vegan options: For creative and delicious vegan recipe ideas as well as tips and assistance on promoting your restaurant's vegan menu items, please contact Compassion Over Killing today. Thank you!

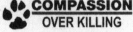

COMPASSION
OVER KILLING

P.O. Box 9773 • Washington, DC 20016 • www.cok.net
info@cok.net • T: 301-891-2458 • F: 301-891-6815

You don't have to motivate personal transformations to get more veg options on menus. COK, led by Erica Meier, has done the strategic analysis to create the four-panel fold-over card at left that advocates can leave on the table after dining out. This small piece shows owners, managers, and chefs how choosing to serve veg options can be fun (profitable), easy, and popular.

Fun

More customers build the bottom line, "fun" for businesses. The information is more credible because the source is an industry publication, *Nation's Restaurant News*.

Easy

COK offers assistance including recipes, tips, and promotion assistance to make it easy. Although the card doesn't mention it, a volunteer vegan chef can work with restaurants that need help. Promotion support includes listing on the website www.VegDC.com.

Popular

Sharing that other restaurants are serving veg options makes it seem like the norm – popular – and implies that those that don't are missing out.

Note also the positive voice on the cover. "I think your restaurant is great…" This tone builds a relationship while a complaining tone could antagonize the chef, owner, or other decision-maker.

See the final section of this chapter, "Bring the Campaign to Your Area" for information on how to order the cards and for other resources on restaurant outreach.

COK also makes offering veg meals easy by suggesting that restaurants try a vegan day or participate in DC's VegWeek to start. Many restaurants keep the new plant-based dishes on the menu when they see the response. More than 125 DC area restaurants display COK's "Proud to Serve Vegetarian & Vegan Meals" decal in their windows.[151]

How to Say Something to Someone Instead of Nothing to Everyone

One size does not fit all. Choose the best people to target and tailor your efforts to them. COK targets its outreach to restaurants that "while not very veg-friendly, could easily alter their menus to include more vegan options."[152] Mercy For Animals takes a similar approach, including in the veg week it adapted from COK.

> The people in the best position to help animals are the omnivores, so that's who we try to reach. Non-vegetarians aren't likely to eat in a veg restaurant. The only veg options they may see in other restaurants are terrible side salads. That's their impression of vegan food, that it's lacking. It's important to work with mainstream restaurants, so people can see delicious vegan options. Plus, with more vegan options on a menu, diners order fewer non-vegan meals, saving more animals.
>
> - Matt Rice, Mercy For Animals

MFA also approaches restaurants by making the business case that they can stand out and attract new customers. By tying its event to World Go Vegan Week, MFA garners more coverage for the restaurants in both local and veg-oriented media. According to Matt:

> We get a lot of good feedback because the restaurants increase business. Traditional restaurants are trying the new items and really enjoying the results. All the comments are very positive, because they're making more money.

Matt notes that the only negative feedback has come from some members of the vegan community who don't understand why MFA promotes restaurants that aren't all veg. While it's important to support and thank veg businesses, if we want to reach beyond the "converted," it's valuable to get veg food into other outlets.

COK's *Guide to Restaurant Outreach* has additional information on how to target efforts to add veg options to menus:

> When choosing a restaurant, consider which establishments may be more open to changes in their menus. In COK's experience, we've found that family-owned or independent restaurants are more apt to take customers' suggestions than are national chains. As independent restaurants are generally free of the red tape associated with national chains, they can not only make decisions

more rapidly but also implement the new offerings immediately, keeping them at the cutting edge of the burgeoning vegetarian market.[153]

I Am Not My Target Audience

You don't think the same way as the people you're trying to influence. Listen to them to understand the best motivators.

My publication *Vegetarian Means Business: Market Strategy and Research Report* also has information you can use to think about how to manage your restaurant outreach and communicate with decision-makers.

> In the National Restaurant Association's "What's Hot in 2011" survey of over 1,500 professional chefs, more than half rated meatless/vegetarian entrees and vegan entrees as a "Hot Trend." Nearly a quarter considered meatless/vegetarian entrees a "Perennial Favorite", while 17% gave that rating to vegan entrees.
>
> Restaurants considering adding veg offerings can also look to larger trends in dining out. Nearly three quarters of chefs rated nutrition/health as a hot trend, making it the 15th most popular item. Nutritionally balanced children's dishes (#4) and fruit/vegetable children's side items (#18) also ranked in the top 20 hottest trends.[154]

You might, for example, tell the manager of a restaurant you approach about how chefs in the "What's Hot in 2011" survey rated vegetarian and vegan entrees. Maybe you'd want to discuss the potential in children's items for establishments that cater to families.

You can also learn more about what might work for a local restaurant by studying menus from similar establishments. For example, if a Chinese menu near you is lacking, see what other Asian restaurants serve, not only in your town but also in other parts of the country. If you can suggest specific vegetable dishes or substituting tofu for meat in Kung Pao chicken and other recipes that are more likely to be manageable for the chef, you're making it easier for the restaurant to respond to your request.

Education Isn't Enough

It takes more than telling people about a problem to inspire them to act. Build your efforts considering product, price, place, and partnerships as well as promotion.

Communicating to restaurants about the potential in veg foods is a great start. Sites such as VegDC.com, VegSeattle.com, VegPortland.com, and others like them are an additional *product/service* that advocates can point out to show how to reach new customers by qualifying for a listing.

Josh Balk uses *product* and *place* in addition to messaging to persuade restaurants. When he visited Hunan Café in Gaithersburg, Maryland, for example, he began by introducing himself and talking about the many people up the street at The HSUS who would be interested in vegan meals. He also brought samples of mock meat *products* that were available from a local restaurant distributor (*place*). In addition, he offered to provide advertising cards called table tents to highlight the new choices to diners (also a *product* of Josh's outreach, even though they're a promotion item for Hunan Café). Manager Raymond Liao said these additional elements made it easier for him to test a vegan menu that the restaurant offers in addition to the regular one.

Voice Matters

How you say it is as important as what you say.

Josh went in several times to see Mr. Liao, offer assistance, and find out whether the veg options were in the works. This follow-up was especially important because Hunan Café is part of a small, regional Washington, DC chain. Mr. Liao not only had to be convinced that veg made sense but also feel motivated enough to take the concept to his supervisor. Josh emphasizes the importance of building relationships, like the one he formed with Mr. Liao.

> **Go in with a big smile. Give out positive energy, so the person doesn't think you're just someone else complaining. You want them to think, "Here's someone nice." Forming the positive bond, going over the issue, and then following up as often and possible in a friendly way… that's how change happens.**

Josh often takes a delicious gift such as chocolate or other vegan treats to meetings to start off on the right foot!

Every time you eat out and ask for a veg option, you have the potential to create a positive impression that inspires change. Gena Hamshaw of

Choosing Raw has advice on how to engage in a way that not only gets you a better meal but also increases the likelihood the restaurant will respond more favorably to future special requests or entreaties to put more veg on the menu.

1) Pick up Your Phone

Sure, you could wait until you arrive at the restaurant to mention that you're vegan. But I wouldn't recommend it. Kitchens are busy, and getting a last minute request for special dining preferences isn't every chef's cup of tea. You can call when you make a reservation, or you can call 24 hours before, but do call. It'll make your dinner better, the chef's night easier, and it'll ensure that the restaurant has no excuse to tell you that no vegan options exist.

2) Be Polite

Yes, the customer is always right, but you're far more likely to secure a nice vegan dish with a sweet attitude than you are with a demanding one. Good manners, a nice tone of voice—these are your secret weapons.

3) Be Realistic

Of course your intention is to have the chef or maître d' promise you a hearty vegan meal. But you should have realistic expectations: a restaurant with nary a vegan option in sight on the website probably isn't going to know how to prepare a really impressive vegan meal.... Nevertheless, it may know how to make a great salad, and it may know how to grill some killer veggies. Be prepared to celebrate whatever options sound good.

- Gena Hamshaw, "Calling Ahead"[155]

Nancy Berkoff of VRG points out how influential you can be with these requests. She suggests targeting local places where they know you and getting your friends involved. She shares the story of a Thai restaurant that got so many special orders that the owner completely restructured the menu. The new menu lists all the dishes as including vegetables and tofu. Diners can add animal proteins. The staff received training on how to serve the valued veg diner clientele, such as asking whether someone does or does not want egg when ordering Pad Thai.

Evaluate, Don't Guess

We have to determine if we're getting results and learn from our experience to do better. Restaurant outreach is fairly easy to evaluate. How many establishments have at least something vegetarian or vegan? How many dishes do they offer? What variety of veg food do they serve? Surveys, including by VRG, that measure what percent of diners order a veg meal out also reflect availability and quality.

The HSUS worked with HRC to tally the number of vegetarian restaurants and compile other indicators in the *Humane Index* (2007). For the twenty-five U.S. metropolitan areas included, there were 530 veg restaurants total. Each metropolitan area had at least three vegetarian restaurants, and five cities on the more progressive west coast averaged 44 each.[156] This study provides a baseline to compare to future counts to assess progress.

Bring the Campaign to Your Area

Many of the organizations mentioned have resources to help you work with local restaurants and other eateries.

COK
• Guide to Restaurant Outreach - http://www.cok.net/lit/rest.php
• To order the restaurant leave-behind cards - http://order.cok.net/restaurant_cards/

MFA
Vegetarian Dining Campaign
http://www.mercyforanimals.org/vegetarian-dining.aspx

VRG
"Encouraging Vegetarian Foods at Concession Stands"
http://www.vrg.org/journal/vj2004issue3/vj2004issue3concession.htm

Choosing Raw
"Calling Ahead"
http://www.choosingraw.com/calling-ahead/

Priority Ventures Group
Vegetarian Means Business: Market Strategy and Research Report
http://priorityventures.com/vegetarian-market-strategy-and-research-report

• • • • • • •

Achieve Impact

1. What reactions or ideas did these examples trigger for you?

2. List one or two ways you could improve what you do based on what you've learned.

Chapter 12

Getting Started

In this chapter:
- **People.** Understanding and empathizing with our audiences is the precursor to success.
  - Revisit the shopping and eating examples in this book, spend time with or research your audience, and complete the *Choosing Your Perspective* activity if helpful.
  - Share these activities with other advocates who would benefit.
- **Priorities.** Focusing on fewer initiatives and using time management practices will create space for you to think more about enhancing your advocacy.
- **Process.** There are many ways to move forward, including developing ideas for a single effort, buddying up with friends, working with a group, or scheduling a retreat.
  - Organizations can consider a marketing committee to bring in additional expertise and resources.
- **Persistence.** Celebrate small victories as you go, and be tenacious in your follow-through.
- **Plan.** Different considerations can help you integrate the ACHIEVEchange system whether you are an individual advocate, organization staff member or volunteer, or an executive director.
- **Progress.** Use these tools to sharpen your advocacy and help others do the same

• • • • • • •

The ACHIEVEchange framework gives you a step-by-step way to strengthen your animal advocacy. To begin getting better results from an existing campaign, program, or personal outreach effort, apply what you've learned to diagnose its strengths and weaknesses. Refer back to each chapter as needed for additional detail to enhance an existing initiative or plan a new one.

Action and Audience
Have you defined a clear action and considered "What's in it for me?" for your audience to do it?

Create Benefits and Cut Barriers

How do you help your audience perceive more benefits than barriers to change?

How to Say Something to Someone Instead of Nothing to Everyone

Have you defined a target audience?

I Am Not My Target Audience

What research have you done to understand the people you're trying to affect?

Education Is Not Enough

How have you deployed the 5Ps of product, price, place, partnerships, and promotion?

Voice Matters

Is the voice you're using the best one to get results?

Evaluate, Don't Guess

What outcomes are you seeing and how can you improve?

Note that you won't always move in a linear fashion through the steps. As you determine your target audience, you'll revisit how to create benefits and cut barriers specific to that group. Your research may reveal that you need to adjust your target. You might come up with new ideas for message, product, price, or other elements that suggest further testing.

Need more help? Here some additional tips to implement the ACHIEVE-change system into your advocacy.

People

The successful animal advocates you've read about here have shown that our work isn't just about animals, it's about people. If we don't understand what matters to the people we're trying to influence, we're unlikely to move them. While we must sometimes be forceful to persuade businesses, organizations, and governments that are resistant to change, that's rarely the best starting point. To be a positive force for animals, we must be a positive force with people.

> The bottom line is that dogs do not adopt or relinquish other dogs. The members of my community are the only ones who can help us make a difference.
>
> - Kim Doner, Humane Society of Lincoln County (New Mexico)

If you are still skeptical on this key point, or even if you'd just benefit from some reinforcement, complete any or all of the following activities. You can share them with colleagues, staff, or volunteers to foster a more people-centered culture.

1. Reread the examples on shopping and eating in the chapter "Why People Don't Get it and What You Can Do." Do you think there are advocates who feel as passionately about these issues as you do about animals? Are they entitled to judge you or treat you badly for not complying with their wishes? What happens if they do? How would you respond?

2. Learn more about your audience. Spend time with people like those you seek to influence. Just observe or ask questions to understand. What matters to them in life? What struggles do they face? What do you have in common? How do they feel about animals? Why might they be opposed to taking the action you're advocating? Reading existing studies can also help ground you in your audience's experience, needs, wants, and views, although usually not as evocatively as in person.

3. Do the *Choosing Your Perspective* exercise below to explore further how your attitude about people impacts your effectiveness. This activity works better with a partner, but you can also do it by yourself.

• • • • • • •

Choosing Your Perspective

Think of an individual, group of people, or organization:
• That you are trying to influence
• Where you have negative feelings

Examples of perspectives you might have about her/him/them:
• I see them as the enemy.
• I think they are bad people.

- I believe they don't care.
- I consider them to be misinformed.
- I have no impression of them.
- I understand them.
- I empathize with them.

Questions to ask:
What perspective do you hold currently?
It does not need to be one in the list above. Those are examples to start your thinking.
- How do you feel and act as a result of holding this perspective?
- What is the impact on your effectiveness?

Is there an alternative perspective you would prefer to hold?
Imagine yourself engaging that person or group with this perspective.
- What would feel different if you held this perspective? How might you act differently?
- How could that change your effectiveness?

What would it take for you to move from where you are now to where you'd like to be?

• • • • • • •

Priorities

Maybe you're thinking, "I just don't have time to do all this," as you consider the ACHIEVEchange system. But as Bruce Friederich of Farm Sanctuary points out:

> Anybody who says they don't have time to reflect on their effectiveness as an advocate really can't afford not to spend time reflecting on their effectiveness as an advocate. In <u>The 7 Habits of Highly Effective People,</u> Stephen Covey makes an extremely strong case that most of us spend our time on things that appear urgent, but are not particularly important. (This is only getting worse with email and Facebook.)

> Many people at the end of the day have been extremely busy, but have nothing lasting they can point to that they have accomplished. Activists really need to be people who are good at time management. A day in which all you do is respond to email is the difference between vast quantities of suffering for animals and being able to alleviate some significant part of that.

See the *Resources* section for books on time management, an important skill for us all.

One way to free up time and to get better results is to do less. Not only less web surfing or busy work but also fewer different campaigns, programs, volunteer roles, or individual efforts. When we spread ourselves thin by pursuing numerous initiatives without enough resources, we don't get very far into any one of them. This is a very common problem for both individual animal advocates and organizations.

> You have to overcome your natural desire to do something on every issue. For organizations, there's so much that can come from supporters, board, staff, and volunteers. Pick an issue and be really focused. Avoid the temptation to cover everything at once.
>
> - Michelle Thew, BUAV

Doing fewer things will not only help you make time for analyzing and planning your efforts but also allow you to become more knowledgeable on your issue(s). Michelle attributes much of BUAV's success in reducing product testing on animals to this focus. She realized that only credible experts would sway the decision-makers in business and government. So rather than having general campaigners working on multiple issues, she's brought in scientists who can address toxicologists, ex-members of Parliament who staff the policy team, and lawyers who carry the day in the courts. By specializing, maintaining a high level of professionalism, and partnering with other members of The European Coalition to End Animal Experiments, BUAV has helped attract hundreds of companies to the Leaping Bunny labeling program for products not tested on animals. Some of these firms even joined the campaign that led to a European Union-wide ban fully effective in 2013. The ban prohibits testing cosmetic products and ingredients on animals as well as selling cosmetic products that have included animal testing.

So what should you focus on? The *Evaluate Don't Guess* chapter covered looking at what you're investing in different issues or programs and what impact that's producing. When I work with organizations on strategic planning, such an assessment, along with determining the group's "distinctive competence" or key strength, is an important part of the project. If you're an advocate working on your own, you can think about time spent against results.

If you have a special talent you bring to the field, that's a good area to consider ... as long as it's something you want to do. For example, Jonathan Balcombe has three biology degrees, including a PhD in ethology, the study of animal behavior. He published a number of valuable scholarly papers on animal suffering in experimentation. However, his real interest was animal pleasure, a topic that doesn't make it into academic and professional journals outside the animal protection realm. Jonathan stopped taking on work related solely to the downsides of animal experimentation. Instead, he has followed his passion and written several successful books on animal pleasure, including The Exultant Ark: A Pictorial Tour of Animal Pleasure. Enthusiastic reviews of his books in The New York Times and other media bring his positive message about animals to a large audience. Jonathan believes that this more buoyant, upbeat approach provides a new way to increase the intrinsic value of animals and raise the moral implications of mistreating them.

Don't know what you would enjoy? Many of the leading animal advocates you've read about started as interns or volunteers. Visit the websites of organizations you know or search online to identify potential opportunities.

Process

There are many ways to turn the ACHIEVEchange system from ideas to action.

- Reread the book thinking about one campaign, program, or outreach effort, noting ideas and follow-ups as you go.
  - An internship or volunteer position with an organization that takes a social marketing approach can provide on-the-job experience to supplement what you've learned.
  - Remember that many of the groups mentioned here offer research, materials, and other information at their websites that you can learn from and use in your own efforts.
- Find a buddy to collaborate with on one campaign or trade ideas on different initiatives you each want to improve.
- Bring together a book group or brainstorming team to talk about the steps and surface ideas about how to apply them to one or more issues.

- Schedule time each day or week to devote to making progress. For example, start with just the *Action and Audience* step in your first session, and then move on to *Create Benefits and Cut Barriers* in the next. If that's too fast, break down each step into smaller activities.
  - If you run a group or organization, consider having a different staff member or volunteer be the topic expert for each step and lead the discussion.
- Plan a retreat or block off time to launch a more in-depth assessment.

Several people interviewed reported using a marketing committee to bring in expertise and resources to the process.

• • • • • • •

Something to Celebrate in New Orleans

Laura Maloney had a tough job facing her when she came in to head Louisiana SPCA after earning her master of business administration degree. The organization was in rough shape financially. It had a poor image, in part due to years of sub-par customer service. She had no marketing staff.

To support her efforts to reposition LA/SPCA, Laura established a marketing committee. She and her team recruited influential marketing experts from the New Orleans area. They targeted people willing to roll up their sleeves and get to work on turning around the organization.

These volunteers helped conduct focus groups. They explored what changes LA/SPCA could make that would engage the public and build trust. Members drew on relationships to bring in other people to participate in developing a new logo, creating new ads, and securing free media placement. The committee and its network spread the word about what the organization was doing and its professional approach. Having people outside the animal protection world as messengers increased LA/SPCA's credibility.

In order to succeed, LA/SPCA needed "people people," not just animal people. Laura and her team emphasized customer service throughout the organization. They wanted visitors and callers to have a positive experience and tell others. Workers behind the scenes needed to provide the same level of responsiveness and support to colleagues.

Creating a more marketing-oriented organization included some bumps along the way. A few board members resigned because they disagreed with approaching shelter management as a business. Some staff members didn't respond to the new expectations, even after coaching, so had to move on.

Being serious about getting results for animals meant getting less, not more, uptight about advocacy. Laura likes to quote a former colleague who advised people to *be of your time*. She elaborates:

> **Learn not to take yourself so seriously. Know what movies are out and what's on the news. That keeps you more grounded in the world, so it doesn't become all about you and your work. Remind yourself that you'll be more effective and able to talk to people outside the movement. Our goal isn't to talk to ourselves. We want to have a big tent and invite people in to have more influence over time.**

As the public started responding positively, staff became more enthusiastic about the new approach. The cultural change and revised marketing materials, along with other efforts such as offsite adoptions and a volunteer day to spruce up the facility, contributed to more animals finding homes. Funding grew because donors saw results and felt confident there would be a return in lives saved for their investment in the organization. Laura feels that without these changes, the organization might have failed during or after the devastation of Hurricane Katrina. Instead, a stronger LA/SPCA has literally weathered the storm and continued as a force for animals in the region.

• • • • • • •

Persistence

Shifts such as viewing people as an audience for change, thinking about benefits and barriers, or reading existing market research can help you get almost immediate improvement in advocacy. The full power you will gain from the ACHIEVEchange system, however, may take longer to play out, just as in developing and leveraging any new skill. Remember to celebrate small victories along the way and keep at it.

It's easy to get distracted and move on to a new approach, issue, or campaign. However, leading advocates emphasize the importance of tenacity and follow-through.

> **Don't get bored, because animals aren't getting bored. It's our responsibility to finish [animal exploitation].**
>
> - Michelle Thew

• • • • • • •

Always be Tenacious – Steve Hindi

Steve Hindi was an avid hunter and fisherman for thirty years. He attended the Hegins pigeon shoot not because of his concerns about animals, but because he felt the event tarnished the reputation of "ethical" hunters like him. When the local hunters said he was no different from them and he spent some time talking with the animal protection advocates, he rethought what he'd been doing.

Steve now brings the same focus, insight, and persistence that he used in hunting to his work helping animals. As founder of Showing Animals Respect and Kindness (SHARK), he's captured riveting footage of bullfighting, rodeos, and pigeon shoots, then used it to prompt change.

These videos become "anti-commercials," if you will, for companies supporting cruelty. After fifty years of sponsoring bullfighting, both Coke and Pepsi stopped when faced with Steve's documentation and the potential damage to their images. It's been more challenging to persuade the companies and even government to get out of rodeo advertising and sponsorship. Many people consider the activity an "American tradition." Steve has nonetheless achieved victories with the Army, the Navy, Starbucks, and Trader Joe's. Coke and Pepsi remain in his sites He continues to bring new footage to light and to call on activists to contact the companies to support change.

Nobody would accuse Steve of being reticent or apologetic about combating cruelty. He's committed to going toe-to-toe with individuals and organizations that harm animals. He's both strategic and persistent.

> You have to be stronger than your opponent, but strength comes in many different forms. If you know anything about martial arts, you know that it's not necessarily how big or strong you are, but how fast and how nimble... You've got to be willing to develop a good plan, be willing to shift as conditions change... and always be tenacious.

• • • • • • •

Plan

The ACHIEVEchange process helps you create the good plan you need to get better results. You can even use the steps to lay out the best way to get yourself or your organization to implement the system. Here are some questions to ask:

Individual Advocates

* What are the most important benefits you would gain by using the ACHIEVEchange system? What barriers do you anticipate?
* How can you overcome these barriers to action?

Executive Directors

* Although you may have the ability to require the ACHIEVEchange system in your organization, how might you persuade people to get on board voluntarily? Remember that you may need to overcome resistance to social marketing's business origin or even the term "marketing."
* What audiences do you have within and across board, staff, volunteers, funders, or other constituents? How can you target key individuals or groups and help them see the benefits to social marketing as being greater than barriers?

Staff and Volunteers

* Do you have responsibilities within your own purview where you can try out the ACHIEVEchange system?
* If not, how might you inspire your work group or immediate supervisor to employ this approach?

Regardless of your current position or level of involvement in animal advocacy, you can create more impact by acting on the lessons learned. The central tenet of marketing and of effective advocacy is seeing people as customers for change who act when they feel the benefits of doing so exceed the barriers. We can only understand how to tip the scales when we understand them by listening. We only have the opportunity to listen when we treat them well enough to engage with us and our ideas. These principles apply from a conversation or a letter through the most complex campaign.

Each of us can implement these core elements at any time.

Progress

More than 80 leading advocates have contributed to this book, because they know how important it is for us to be as effective as possible when helping animals. You have the opportunity not only to use what you have learned but also to share these approaches with others. Together we can elevate our collective efforts and do more for animals faster. Here are just a few things you can do:

- Share your success stories with me at cginsberg@priorityventures.com. Examples of what's working provide powerful lessons. I'd love to hear what you're doing and provide the best examples to others.
- Talk about key points you've learned with fellow advocates in blogs, on Facebook or Twitter, or in presentations. Join the conversation at Facebook.com/AnimalImpact and invite others to do so.
- Get the book into more hands as gifts; in your book club; at the library; to staff, volunteers, and board members; via your website; or through your organization's newsletter or store. For pricing on volume orders, please visit Animal-Impact.com/volume.

The scope of animal suffering is so vast that our job as advocates may seem overwhelming. As in any job, having the right tools makes a big difference. If you try to slice a tomato with a dull knife, you'll end up with a juicy mess. You need a fine edge to cut through cleanly. The ACHIEVEchange system gives you that fine edge to cut through resistance to change.

As Heidi Prescott said in the foreword, "we share a passion for animals." She and I also have a passion for using these tools to improve effectiveness. I hope that you now share some of that passion and will use the ACHIEVEchange system to move the world.

• • • • • • •

Achieve Impact

> Excellence is an art won by training and habituation. We do not act rightly because we have virtue or excellence, but we rather have those because we have acted rightly. We are what we repeatedly do. Excellence, then, is not an act, but a habit.
>
> – Aristotle

1. How will you implement the ACHIEVEchange system?

2. In what ways do you want to share what you've learned with others?

3. "A" is for Action and Audience. What one action can you take TODAY to move forward?

About the Author

Caryn Ginsberg has spent more than a decade helping animal protection advocates utilize proven strategy and marketing approaches to get better results. She has worked with the ASPCA, The HSUS, PetSmart Charities, Farm Sanctuary, Humane Farm Animal Care, and RedRover, among others. She has served on boards of directors and advisory boards, including for the Institute for Humane Education and the Humane Research Council. Clients and colleagues appreciate Caryn's ability to get to the heart of what matters, focus on what's actionable, and generate new ideas.

As a classroom instructor, she has led marketing courses in the MBA program at Johns Hopkins University. She also taught social marketing and strategic management in a joint program of Johns Hopkins and Humane Society University (HSU). Her online courses for HSU include *Building an Effective Campaign: Research and Planning* (co-developed with Heidi Prescott); *Social Marketing; Statistics Surveys and Scorecards;* and *Measuring Effectiveness.*

A popular speaker, Caryn has presented at the *Taking Action for Animals* conference, the *Animal Rights National Conference,* and *Animal Care Expo* as well as meetings of Animal Grantmakers and the National Council on Pet Population Study & Policy. She is co-author with the ASPCA's Bert Troughton of *Making Plans to Make a Difference: Business Planning for Shelters to Inspire, Mobilize, and Sustain Change.* She has also written articles for *The Animals' Agenda, Vegetarian Journal,* and *Executive Update.*

Caryn holds an MBA from the Stanford Graduate School of Business and an A.B. in economics/mathematics from Dartmouth College, where she played varsity ice hockey. She earned an advanced certificate in marketing design from Sessions College for Professional Design. Her favorite animals are sheep, and her backyard is full of birds and squirrels who let her know when the feeders are empty.

To bring Caryn's expertise to your organization, program, campaign, or event, please contact her at cginsberg@priorityventures.com.

Photos of Caryn Ginsberg by Tomerlin Photography

Resources

Social Marketing and Social Change

Philip Kotler and Nancy R. Lee, Social Marketing: Influencing Behaviors for Good (Los Angeles: Sage Publications, 2011)

Alan R. Andreasen, Marketing Social Change: Changing Behavior to Promote Health, Social Development, and the Environment (San Francisco: Jossey-Bass Publishers, 1995)

Chip Heath and Dan Heath, Made to Stick: Why Some Ideas Survive and Others Die (New York: Random House, Inc., 2007)

Chip Heath and Dan Heath, Switch: How to Change Things When Change Is Hard (New York, Random House, Inc., 2010)

Andy Goodman, *Why Bad Ads Happen to Good Causes: And How to Ensure They Won't Happen to Yours*, http://www.agoodmanonline.com/bad_ads_good_causes/

By Animal Advocates

Heidi Prescott and Caryn Ginsberg, *Building an Effective Campaign: Research and Planning*, Humane Society University online course, http://humanesocietyuniversity.org/academics/sce/courseinfo/coursepage.aspx?id=131

Nick Cooney, Change of Heart: What Psychology Can Teach Us About Spreading Social Change (New York: Lantern Books, 2011)

Hillary Rettig, The Lifelong Activist: How to Change the World Without Losing Your Way (New York: Lantern Books, 2006)

Josephine Bellaccomo, Move the Message: Your Guide to Making a Difference and Changing the World (New York: Lantern Books, 2004)

Matt Ball and Bruce Friedrich, The Animal Activist's Handbook (Brooklyn: Lantern Books, 2009)

Peter Singer, <u>Ethics into Action: Henry Spira and the Animal Rights Movement</u> (Lanham, Maryland: Rowman & Littlefield Publishers, 1998)

Melanie Joy, <u>Strategic Action for Animals</u> (New York: Lantern Books, 2008)

Market Research and Evaluation

The Humane Research Council, http://humaneresearch.org and Humane-Spot, http://humanespot.org

Alan R. Andreasen, <u>Marketing Research that Won't Break the Bank</u> (San Francisco, Jossey-Bass, 2002)

W.K. Kellogg Foundation Evaluation Handbook, 1998, http://www.wkkf.org/knowledge-center/resources/2010/W-K-Kellogg-Foundation-Evaluation-Handbook.aspx

Social Media

The Social Animal, http://www.thesocialanimal.com/

Vegan Mainstream, http://www.veganmainstream.com/

Time Management

David Allen, <u>Getting Things Done: The Art of Stress Free Productivity</u> (New York: Penguin Group, 2001)

Stephen R. Covey, <u>The 7 Habits of Highly Effective People</u>, (New York: Free Press, 2004)

Endnotes

1. "Tactics," http://management.about.com/cs/generalmanagement/g/tactics.htm
2. "Strategy," http://en.wikipedia.org/wiki/Strategy
3. http://www.animalsandsociety.org/assets/library/449_s1015.pdf
4. Comment on Bert Troughton's, "Squandering Resources," *Shelters' Edge,: The ASPCApro Blog,* September 20, 2011, http://www.aspcapro.org/blog/2011/09/squandering-resources/
5. Humane Research Council, "Humane Trends" and via email, from U.S. Department of Agriculture statistics.
6. Rich Avanzino, President of Maddie's Fund, quoted by Cathy M. Rosenthal in "Progress Made for Animals since 1970," *San Antonio Express News,* October 21, 2010, http://blog.mysanantonio.com/animals/2010/10/progress-made-for-animals-since-1970/
7. U.S. Fish & Wildlife Service, http://www.fws.gov/hunting/huntstat.html
8. U.S. Fish & Wildlife Service data compiled by The Fund for Animals, reported by In Defense of Animals, http://www.idausa.org/facts/hunting.html
9. Humane Research Council, "Humane Trends," from U.S. Department of Agriculture statistics, http://usda.mannlib.cornell.edu/MannUsda/viewDocumentInfo.do?documentID=1497 and http://usda.mannlib.cornell.edu/MannUsda/viewDocumentInfo.do?documentID=1097
10. American Pet Products Association, "Industry Statistics & Trends," http://www.americanpetproducts.org/press_industrytrends.asp
11. Based on data in reports at http://guidestar.org and at organization websites
12. Fur Information Council of America, "FICA Facts," http://www.fur.org/fica-facts/
13. Dan Eggen, "Another Victory for the Bulletproof NRA," *The Washington Post,* June 17, 2010, http://www.washingtonpost.com/wp-dyn/content/article/2010/06/16/AR2010061605341.html
14. Jeff Manning and Kevin Lane Keller, "Making Advertising Work: How GOT MILK? Marketing Stopped a 20 Year Sales Decline," *Marketing Management,* January/February 2003, 19
15. Based on data in reports at http://guidestar.org, at organization websites and from author estimates
16. Chris Cade, " Fail Your Way to Success," *Getting Things Changed,* ecourse, part 6 of 7
17. Peter Singer, Ethics into Action, (Lanham, Maryland: Rowman & Littlefield Publishers, Inc., 1998), x
18. Christoph A. Reinhardt, Alternatives To Animal Testing: New Ways In The Biomedical Sciences, Trends And Progress (Weinheim, Germany: Wiley-VCH, 1994), 7
19. Bruce Friedrich, "Effective Advocacy: Stealing from the Corporate Playbook" http://arzone.ning.com/profiles/blogs/effective-advocacy-stealing
20. http://uncultured.com/, shared by Alexandra Bornkessel
21. http://invisiblepeople.tv/, shared by Alexandra Bornkessel
22. http://www.ethicsbasedmarketing.net/home.html and via email
23. Philip Kotler, Ned Roberto and Nancy Lee, *Social Marketing: Improving the Quality of Life* (Thousand Oaks, California: Sage Publications Inc., 2002), 5
24. Philip Kotler and Gerald Zaltman, "Social Marketing: An Approach to Planned Social Change," *Journal of Marketing,* Vol. 35, July 1971, 3-12
25. Kathy Savesky via email
26. Kathy Savesky via email
27. Alex Hershaft, *National Animal Rights Conference 2009,* audio recording
28. Kathy Savesky via email
29. Mike Newton-Ward, "Widgets, Tweets, AND 4-Ps – Oh My! Differentiating Social Media and Social Marketing," Fall 2009, http://www.slideshare.net/sm1guru/social-media-vs-social-marketing-for-slideshare-2845992
30. "B-Side Chats: Interview With Mark Horvath, A Man Who Gives Homeless People Across the Country a Place on Camera," http://blisted.breakthrough.tv

31.   Kathy Savesky, "Selling Your Organization's Messages," *Animal Sheltering*, January-February 1999, http://www.animalsheltering.org/resource_library/magazine_articles/jan_feb_1999/selling_your_organizations_messages.html

32.   * Based on Quote by Jay Conrad Levinson, Guerrilla Marketing (New York: Mariner Books, 1994)

33.   Lakshmi Challa , "Impact of Textiles and Clothing Industry on Environment: Approach Towards Eco-Friendly Textiles,", www.fibre2fashion.com

34.   Ruth Domoney, "Briefing on the Chinese Garment Industry," www.fibre2fashion.com

35.   Sharanya Krishna Prasad via email

36.   Kartick Satyanarayan via email

37.   " Project makes new lives for people and bears," http://www.wspa-international.org/wspaswork/bears/dancingbears/new_lives.aspx

38.   Melanie Joy, Strategic Action for Animals (New York: Lantern Books, 2008), 65

39.   http://www.dogchannel.com/dog-news/creator-of-unique-dog-adoption-program.aspx

40.   Emily Weiss, "Get Over Yourself," *Shelters' Edge,: The ASPCApro Blog* , April 7, 2011, http://www.aspcapro.org/blog/2011/04/get-over-yourself/

41.   Ipsos Marketing, *PetSmart Charities A&U Barriers*, May 27, 2009, slide 15 http://www.petsmartcharities.org/resources/resources-documents/PetSmartCharities_Research_AUBarriers.pdf

42.   http://www.richmondspca.org/page.aspx?pid=255

43.   Maddie's Fund, *The Shelter Pet Project By the Numbers - And Something More*, http://www.maddiesfund.org/resource_library/the_shelter_pet_project_by_the_numbers.html

44.   http://www.aspcapro.org/meet-your-match-canine-ality-graphics.php

45.   Emily Weiss, "Meet Your Match Saves Lives," *Shelters' Edge,: The ASPCApro Blog* , May 27, 2010, http://www.aspcapro.org/blog/2010/05/meet-your-match-saves-lives/

46.   Striking at the Roots, " Josh Balk: Helping Campuses and Companies Reduce Cruelty," http://strikingattheroots.wordpress.com/tag/josh-balk/

47.   "Appalling Animal Abuse and Food Safety Threats at Top Egg Producer," http://www.humanesociety.org/news/press_releases/2010/11/cal-maine_111710.html

48.   WSPA, *Practical Alternatives to Industrial Farming in Latin America*, http://www.wspa.org.uk/Images/PracticalAlternativesReport_tcm9-2616.pdf

49.   WSPA, *The facts about our food: Intensive poultry farming*, http://www.wspa.org.uk/Images/PoultryLeaflet_tcm9-2615.pdf

50.   http://www.humanesociety.org/issues/confinement_farm/facts/battery_cage_photos.html

51.   Singer, Ethics into Action, 52

52.   Philip Kotler, Joel Shalowitz, and Robert J. Stevens, Strategic Marketing For Health Care Organizations: Building a Customer-Driven Health System (San Francisco: Jossey Bass, 2008)

53.   Shannon Bryant, "Motivations to Eat Healthy Vary by Generation," *Marketing Forecast*, http://www.marketingforecast.com/archives/10417. I also shared research findings from the National Cattleman's Beef Association at the Summit for the Animals meeting that taste, nutrition, safety, convenience, and value were the factor consumers consider in beef purchases. That study no longer appears to be publicly available online nor do I have the citation. This 2008 presentation by the Director Of Retail for Certified Angus Beef LLC reports the same consumer expectations on slide 19, www.ppttube.com/presentations/com_angus.ppt

54.   Andrea Sachs, "VegFest makes a case for flavor without animal products," *The Washington Post*, September 29, 2011, http://www.washingtonpost.com/blogs/all-we-can-eat/post/vegfest-makes-a-case-for-flavor-without-animal-products/2011/09/28/gIQA1gIj5K_blog.html

55.   "Profile: Dumb Friends League," http://denver.jobing.com/company_profile.asp?i=15702

56.   Brenda Shoss, "Be Their Voice: Essence of a Compelling Letter," http://www.kinshipcircle.org/columns_articles/0042.html

57.   ASPCA, *More Hands to Save More Lives*, http://www.aspcapro.org/mydocuments/aspca_ebook_tallahassee.pdf

58.   Emily Garman, How to be an Advocate on Facebook," *Taking Action for Animals* conference, July 17, 2011

59. Mike Newton-Ward, "Social Marketing—'Apropos of the...Snow,'" March 9, 2009, http://www.socialmarketingpanorama.com/social_marketing_panorama/2009/03/social-marketingapropos-of-thesnow.html

60. "Fur-Free Retailers and Designers," http://www.humanesociety.org/assets/pdfs/fur/fur-free_retailers.pdf

61. Charles Tomkovick, co-instructor, in Humane Society University class

62. Josephine Bellaccomo, Move the Message: Your Guide to Making a Difference and Changing the World (New York: Lantern Books, 2004), 44-45

63. James Hettinger, "There Ought to Be a LAW . . . and here's how to get one passed," *All Animals*, March / April 2009, 7

64. The HSUS, "Our Guide to Help Chained Dogs," http://humanesociety.org/issues/chaining_tethering/tips/chaining_guide.html

65. Chip Heath and Dan Heath, Switch: How to Change Things When Change Is Hard (New York, Random House, Inc., 2010), 259

66. Maura Mitchell, "Carbon Footprint Discourages Green Behavior," http://www.brandology.com/newsletter/informaction20110512.htm

67. Karly Gould, "Bringing Humane Education to the Classroom," *Journal*, http://redrover.org/documents/UAN_Journal_Summer_2011.pdf

68. Alan R. Andreasen, Marketing Social Change: Changing Behavior to Promote Health, Social Development, and the Environment (San Francisco: Jossey-Bass Publishers, 1995), 277-280

69. "Campaign for Red Knot Habitat Preservation," http://rareconservation.org/article/san-antonio-bay-argentina

70. "Modern Alternatives to Dissection," http://www.peta.org/issues/animals-used-for-experimentation/alternatives-to-dissection.aspx

71. P.J. Smith, "Fashion Student Lizette Avineri Chooses Compassion," http://www.humanesociety.org/news/news/2011/05/student_avineri_furfree_052411.html

72. Steve Freiss, "Feeling Pooped by Pigeons, Cities Try Bird Birth Control," AOLNews, http://www.aolnews.com/2010/07/02/feeling-pooped-by-pigeons-cities-try-bird-birth-control/

73. "What is the Tipping Point?", http://www.gladwell.com/tippingpoint/

74. "Interview with Erica Meier of Compassion Over Killing," *The Vegan Culinary Experience*, June 2009, http://www.cok.net/inthenews/20090601.php

75. Humane Research Council, *Vegetarian Consumers Trends*, http://www.cultivateresearch.com/our_research.htm

76. Humane Research Council, *Advocating Meat Reduction and Vegetarianism to Adults in the U.S.*, http://HumaneSpot.org/system/files/HRC_Veg_Study_2007.pdf

77. Euromonitor International, "The War on Meat: How Low-meat and No-meat Diets are Impacting Consumer Markets" http://www.euromonitor.com/the-war-on-meat-how-low-meat-and-no-meat-diets-are-impacting-consumer-markets/report, 2011 via Humane Research Council

78. Esther Mechler, "Creating Spay/Neuter Programs that Work," November 29, 2004, http://www.bestfriends.org/archives/forums/112904spay.html

79. "Greens Leading Way Against Chicken Cages," http://www.voxy.co.nz/politics/greens-leading-way-against-chicken-cages/5/103340

80. Ibid.

81. http://en.wikipedia.org/wiki/Green_Party_of_Aotearoa_New_Zealand and http://en.wikipedia.org/wiki/ACT_New_Zealand

82. http://dawnwatch.com

83. "News: Survey for National Vegetarian Week," http://www.mmr-research.com/news/survey-for-national-vegetarian-week/

84. Hal Herzog, "Why Do Most Vegetarians Go Back To Eating Meat?" *Psychology Today*,, June 20 2011, http://www.psychologytoday.com/blog/animals-and-us/201106/why-do-most-vegetarians-go-back-eating-meat

85. Jack Norris, "Response to Paleosister," http://jacknorrisrd.com/?p=1656

86. Humane Research Council, *Attitudes and Behaviors Relating to Fur*, August 2003 (unpublished)

87. Humane Research Council, *Animal Tracker – Wave 2*, March 31, 2009, http://www.humaneresearch.org/content/animal-tracker-wave-2-march-2009

88. Ibid.

89. Bob Leonard, "Saving Habitats and Lives: Seven Steps to Winning for Wildlife," *Beaversprite*, Winter 2006, http://www.beaversww.org/beavers-and-wetlands/articles/saving-habitats-and-lives/

90. Ibid.

91. " Voters Protect Pigs in Florida, Ban Cockfighting in Oklahoma," November 6, 2002, http://www.humanesociety.org/news/news/2002/florida_gestation_crates_OK_cockfight_110602.html

92. http://www.FiXiT-foundation.org/about.html

93. Chip Heath and Dan Heath, <u>Made to Stick: Why Some Ideas Survive and Others Die</u> (New York: Random House, Inc., 2007)

94. "Wish upon a Whisker Wednesday," http://www.edmontonhumanesociety.com/index.php?option=com_content&view=article&id=408&Itemid=59

95. Heather McIntyre, "EHS Seeing an Influx of Animals," May 10, 2011, *Metro Edmonton*, http://www.metronews.ca/edmonton/local/article/855868--ehs-seeing-an-influx-of-animals

96. Kotler, Roberto, and Lee, <u>Social Marketing</u>, 244

97. Michael D. Mullins, "Pets for Life NYC saves 10,000 Pets from Abandonment," *The New York Companion*, Winter 2010, https://www.newyorkcompanion.com/2010_Winter_PetsforLife.html

98. Ibid.

99. Carrie Allan, " Brandishing The Long Arm Of The Law: Working With Police To End Dogfighting," *Animal Sheltering*, Jul-Aug 2006, http://www.animalsheltering.org/resource_library/magazine_articles/jul_aug_2006/working_with_police_to_end_dogfighting.html

100. Ibid.

101. Regina Malone, " A 'Flip' Chat With...Danielle Brigida, Digital Marketing Manager, National Wildlife Federation," *Philantopic*, April 28, 2011, http://pndblog.typepad.com/pndblog/2011/04/a-flip-chat-with-danielle-brigidadlife-federation.html

102. Bert Troughton and Caryn Ginsberg, *Making Plans to Make A Difference: Business Planning For Shelters To Inspire, Mobilize And Sustain Change,* http://www.aspcaonlinestore.com/products/102031-making-plans-to-make-a-difference

103. Anthony Bellotti, "Strategy and Message Development 101," *Taking Action for Animals conference*, July 16, 2011

104. Anthony Bellotti, *Building an Effective Campaign: Research and Planning*, Humane Society University course, http://humanesocietyuniversity.org/academics/sce/courseinfo/coursepage.aspx?id=131

105. Anthony Bellotti, "Strategy and Message Development for Animal Advocacy," http://HumaneSpot.org/system/files/Article+-+Strategy+and+Message+Development+-+Formatted.pdf

106. Chip Heath and Dan Heath, <u>Made to Stick</u>

107. Humane Research Council, *Animal Tracker – Wave 2*

108. Jill Howard Church, "To Serve and Protect: Sergeant Sherry Slaughter," in <u>Speaking Out for Animals: True Stories About Real People who Rescue Animals</u>, ed. Kim W. Stallwood (New York: Lantern Books, New York, 2001)

109. Hilary Rettig, <u>The Lifelong Activist</u> (New York: Lantern Books, 2006), http://lifelongactivist.com/part-v-managing-your-relationship-with-others/17-why-you're-not-getting-through/

110. Will Bowen, <u>Complaint Free World: How to Stop Complaining and Start Enjoying the Life You Always Wanted</u> (New York: DoubleDay, 2007), 109-110

111. Joy, 112

112. Matt Ball and Bruce Friedrich, <u>The Animal Activist's Handbook</u> (Brooklyn: Lantern Books, 2009)

113. Sherry Gilkin, *Teaching for Transformation: A Handbook for Adult Educators*, cited in Marsha Rakestraw's "Humane Educator's Toolbox: New Sample Master's Theses from IHE Students," http://humaneconnectionblog.blogspot.com/2011/05/humane-educators-toolbox-new-sample.html

114. Mark Hawthorne, "Transforming People through Humane Education," http://strikingattheroots.wordpress.com/2010/08/08/transforming-people-through-humane-education/

115. Hershaft, *National Animal Rights Conference 2009*

116. Tim Sansbury, "One Quarter of U.S. Consumers Far More Likely to Spread the Word About a Bad Experience than a Good One," http://www.colloquy.com/press_release_view.asp?xd=92).

117. Ipsos Marketing, *PetSmart Charities A&U Barriers*, slides 13, 15, 18, 24, 50.

118. "Full Year Asilomar Report for 2009" and "Full Year Asilomar Report for 2010," http://www.bayareahumanesociety.com/about.html

119. "What a Difference a Year Makes," http://awlahawk.org/2011/09/14/what-a-difference-a-year-makes/

120. "Child Labor in U.S. History," http://www.continuetolearn.uiowa.edu/laborctr/child_labor/about/us_history.html

121. "The Fight for Women's Suffrage," http://www.history.com/topics/the-fight-for-womens-suffrage

122. Che Green, "The Death of Animal Rights," http://www.humanespot.org/node/2790.

123. Alex Felsinger via email

124. "Pay Per View," http://www.farmusa.org/PPV/

125. "Video Outreach," http://www.vegfund.org/video-intro.html. International advocates not eligible for Pay Per View, but may qualify for other video outreach that does not involve cash payments to the viewer. Per email from Adam Orand

126. "Ancient Greece and Rome, Lucius Annaeus Seneca," http://www.ivu.org/history/greece_rome/seneca.html

127. "United Animal Nations," http://en.wikipedia.org/wiki/United_Animal_Nations

128. Frank Hamilton, by email and in-person, from Hillsborough County Animal Services (Florida), monthly reports June 2001-May 2011

129. Fur Information Council of America, "FICA Facts"

130. Melissa Magsaysay, "Faux fur, fur real," *Los Angeles Times*, August 28, 2011, http://www.latimes.com/features/image/la-ig-highfaux-20110828,0,6153472.story

131. "FTSE 100 Index," http://en.wikipedia.org/wiki/FTSE_100_Index

132. Meeting with Sharanya Krishna Prasad, September 15, 2011

133. Bert Troughton, "Squandering Resources," *Shelters' Edge: The ASPCApro Blog*, September 20, 2011, http://www.aspcapro.org/blog/2011/09/squandering-resources/

134. "Christine Benninger," http://ecorner.stanford.edu/author/christine_benninger

135. Heidi Prescott and Caryn Ginsberg, *Building an Effective Campaign: Research and Planning*, Humane Society University course, http://humanesocietyuniversity.org/academics/sce/courseinfo/coursepage.aspx?id=131

136. Maria Halkias, "Neiman Marcus settles Humane Society's fur lawsuit for $25,000," *The Dallas Morning News*, February 1, 2010, http://www.dallasnews.com/business/headlines/20100201-Neiman-Marcus-settles-Humane-Society-s-8830.ece

137. *W.K. Kellogg Foundation Evaluation Handbook*, http://www.wkkf.org/knowledge-center/resources/2010/W-K-Kellogg-Foundation-Evaluation-Handbook.aspx

138. *Gulf Coast Pet Research Project: Phase 1*, http://www.animalsheltering.org/programs_and_services/spay_neuter/The HSUS-gulf-phase-1-final-public.pdf

139. Ibid.

140. Purina, *State of the American Pet*, cited in *Gulf Coast Pet Research Project: Phase 1*, slide11, http://www.animalsheltering.org/programs_and_services/spay_neuter/The HSUS-gulf-phase-1-final-public.pdf

141. Joshua M. Frank and Pamela Carlisle-Frank, "Sterilization and Contextual Factors of Abandonment: A Study of Pet Overpopulation," http://www.firepaw.org/wpsandc.html

142. *Messaging Spay/Neuter, Lessons from the Gulf Coast Spay/Neuter Campaign*, http://www.animalsheltering.org/programs_and_services/spay_neuter/messaging-spay-neuter-report-_-final.pdf

143. Ibid.

144. Ibid.
145. Ibid.
146. Ibid.
147. "Our Story," http://www.unchaindogs.net/our_story.shtml.
148. Betsy McFarland, "Bridging the Gulf: A Brighter Future for Animals," http://www.humanesociety.org/news/news/2010/08/bridging_gulf_081010.html
149. Amanda Arrington, "Helping Pets in the Gulf," http://www.humanesociety.org/news/news/2010/03/helping_pets_gulf_coast_spay_neuter_032210.html
150. Interview with Reed Mangels
151. "Restaurant Outreach Program," http://www.cok.net/camp/rest/
152. Ibid.
153. " COK's Guide to Restaurant Outreach," http://www.cok.net/lit/rest.php
154. "Chef Survey: What's Hot in 2011," http://www.restaurant.org/pdfs/research/whats_hot_2011.pdf
155. Gena Hamshaw, "Calling Ahead," http://www.choosingraw.com/calling-ahead/
156. "Humane Eats," http://www.humaneindex.org/

Index

Made in the USA
Charleston, SC
09 January 2012